DIRECTIONS FOR HIGHER EDUCATION

Martin Kramer, *University of California, Berkeley*
EDITOR-IN-CHIEF

The Changing Dimensions of Student Aid

Jamie P. Merisotis
Higher Education Consultant

EDITOR

Number 74, Summer 1991

JOSSEY-BASS INC., PUBLISHERS, San Francisco

MAXWELL MACMILLAN INTERNATIONAL PUBLISHING GROUP
New York • Oxford • Singapore • Sydney • Toronto

THE CHANGING DIMENSIONS OF STUDENT AID
Jamie P. Merisotis (ed.)
New Directions for Higher Education, no. 74
Volume XIX, number 2
Martin Kramer, Editor-in-Chief

Microfilm copies of issues and articles are available in 16mm and 35mm, as well as microfiche in 105mm, through University Microfilms Inc., 300 North Zeeb Road, Ann Arbor, Michigan 48106.

LC 85-644752 ISSN 0271-0560 ISBN 1-55542-790-1

NEW DIRECTIONS FOR HIGHER EDUCATION is part of The Jossey-Bass Higher and Adult Education Series and is published quarterly by Jossey-Bass Inc., Publishers (publication number USPS 990-880). Second-class postage paid at San Francisco, California, and at additional mailing offices. Postmaster: Send address changes to Jossey-Bass Inc., Publishers, 350 Sansome Street, San Francisco, California 94104.

EDITORIAL CORRESPONDENCE should be sent to the Editor-in-Chief, Martin Kramer, 2807 Shasta Road, Berkeley, California 94708.

Cover photograph and random dot by Richard Blair/Color & Light © 1990.

Printed on acid-free paper in the United States of America.

Contents

Editor's Notes 1
Jamie P. Merisotis

1. The Roots of Federal Student Aid Policy 3
Janet S. Hansen
Student aid's conceptual and operational roots help explain recent program changes and current policy dilemmas.

2. The Shifting Roles of Parents and Students 21
Janet S. Hansen
The 1980s saw a renewed emphasis on parental and student responsibility for financing higher education, as federal aid programs lagged behind college costs.

3. Strengthening and Refining the Federal-State-Institutional Partnership 33
Jamie P. Merisotis
A strengthened student aid partnership needs to use existing funds more efficiently, regulate how students receive aid more effectively, and delineate the rights and responsibilities of each of the major partners more adequately.

4. Simplification of Need Analysis and Aid Delivery: Imperatives and Opportunities 43
Brian K. Fitzgerald
Complexity of the current application and aid delivery system is helping to motivate efforts to simplify the process that culminates in the awarding of student aid.

5. Constant Response to Change: The Role of the Financial Aid Office 65
Natala K. Hart
The many changes that have taken place in the student aid system in recent years have necessitated a series of operational and programmatic adjustments for financial aid administrators and their offices.

6. Where Do We Go from Here: Looking Beyond Student Aid and Access to Persistence 75
Oscar F. Porter
Financial aid is one of several variables that policymakers must consider in any effort to improve college persistence.

Index 91

Editor's Notes

As we enter the decade of the 1990s, student financial aid in America is at a crossroads. Programs that for nearly two decades enjoyed nearly constant growth and expansion—and that were extremely well received by policymakers, educators, students, and the public at large—are now being called into question. Questions about the effectiveness of programs, the targeting of resources to those who most deserve assistance, and the need for greater indicators of programmatic success are just a few of those being asked by even the staunchest of student aid advocates.

The reasons for this public reexamination of a national student aid policy are many. The failure of programs to increase significantly the participation and success of minority and disadvantaged students, the growing dollar amount of student loan defaults, the expanding use of programs by students attending private vocational (proprietary) schools, and many other factors have been cited as contributing to the need for a comprehensive review of progress to date and prospects for future success. In many cases these factors are directly related to budgetary imperatives that, particularly at the federal level, have grown more and more pressing as the programs have grown in size and importance.

There is certainly a danger in trying to arrive at general conclusions about programs that—counting federal, state, and institutional sources—award more than $25 billion a year in student aid. Failure to acknowledge the many accomplishments of these programs may compromise the foundation upon which a tremendous educational investment has been made. The consequence could be disastrous for the long-term viability of student assistance and its many worthy goals. However, the future of higher education could also benefit from these discussions. A reasonable discussion concerned with strengthening existing programs and policies and creating new incentives and opportunities for equal educational opportunity would be a positive force on both programs and the students who participate in them.

A review of recent changes in student aid can provide a context for the reform-minded discussions that will be taking place over the next few years. In particular, a better grasp of the conceptual and operational shifts that have occurred in the past ten years can illuminate the challenges facing colleges, students, and the nation at large in the coming decade. The purpose of this volume, then, is to provide college administrators and others with a broad sense of how and why student aid has changed and what these changes portend. Our goal is to offer a better understanding of and appreciation for the difficult and complex issues confronting those devoted to improving the prospects of equal educational opportunity for all students.

In the first chapter, Janet S. Hansen offers a historical overview of the federal approach to student aid. Included is a discussion of the forces driving federal policy and the effects they have had on aid recipients and amounts.

The second chapter, also by Hansen, zeroes in on the primary recipients of aid—parents and students. Both groups saw their role in paying for college change fairly dramatically in the past decade as a result of such factors as rising college costs, a shift in federal support from grants to loans, and the failure of family income to keep pace with cost increases.

The third chapter (by the editor) explores issues related to who provides aid and how those providers interact and coordinate their efforts. The author describes the need for a greater partnership among the major players and makes specific suggestions for stating rights and responsibilities more explicitly and improving cooperation among the partners.

In the fourth chapter, Brian K. Fitzgerald offers a detailed look at the aid application process. This process, which is generally known to be complex and confusing, has been widely discussed as a barrier to access for needy students. Opportunities to address the shortcomings of the need-analysis and delivery systems are included in this chapter.

The fifth chapter, by Natala K. Hart, brings the discussion close to home for campus administrators by examining the many changes that have taken place in campus financial aid offices in recent years. The many operational and programmatic difficulties currently facing financial aid administrators as well as the prospects for future relief are analyzed.

In the final chapter, Oscar F. Porter extends the view of financial aid by exploring its effects on not only access to higher education but also persistence and student success. The role that financial aid might play in improving student achievement represents a revised, relatively unexplored frontier for student aid and could be a major emphasis for policymakers and college administrators for the coming decade.

Jamie P. Merisotis
Editor

Jamie P. Merisotis is a higher education consultant in Washington, D.C., who specializes in issues related to the financing of higher education.

Student aid's conceptual and operational roots help explain recent program changes and current policy dilemmas.

The Roots of Federal Student Aid Policy

Janet S. Hansen

Federal student aid policy at any moment in time indicates society's answer to a fundamental question: how should the costs of higher education be distributed? Johnstone (1986) has identified four possible partners who can share the burden of financing higher education: taxpayers (both state and federal), parents, students, and higher education institutions and their philanthropic sponsors.

Reflecting on the situation in the 1980s, he has observed that colleges and universities in the United States rely on more diverse sources of revenue and share the burden more equally than in many other countries. American taxpayers bear relatively less responsibility than many of their foreign counterparts for the direct support of institutions, all of which charge some student fees and some of which are privately rather than publicly sponsored. Parents and students have the primary obligation to meet tuition charges and living expenses, although institutions and state and federal taxpayers have gradually assumed a portion of this burden as well through the programs we call student financial aid. One consequence of shared responsibility for financing is that the United States is able and willing to support unparalleled access to postsecondary schooling.

The gradual evolution of taxpayer, especially federal taxpayer, responsibility for student aid is the subject of this chapter. The changing face of

---

Portions of this chapter are based on an earlier article by the author. See J. S. Hansen, "Cost-Sharing in Higher Education: The United States Experience." In M. Woodhall (ed.), *Financial Support for Students: Grants, Loans or Graduate Tax?* London: Kogan Page (in association with the Institute of Education, University of London), 1989.

student aid, in both its programmatic and administrative aspects, is largely the story of how the federal government became the nation's major provider of direct support to students and the implications of this growth for institutions, students, and campus administrators. This chapter traces the development of federal student aid programs and procedures and suggests the policy issues that are on the public agenda as we enter the 1990s. Subsequent chapters in this volume examine the implications of these programs, procedures, and policy issues for the producers and consumers of postsecondary education.

A Brief History of Federal Student Aid

Before the mid-1960s, the federal government was only a minor partner in the enterprise of paying for college. Parents and students bore most of the burden of postsecondary expenses. What financial assistance was available came mostly from colleges themselves. A few states had grant and/or loan programs, and the federal government had put its toe into the water when it created loans for financially needy students as part of the post-Sputnik National Defense Education Act in 1958. (The lineal descendants of NDEA loans are now called Perkins Loans, in honor of former congressman Carl D. Perkins.) There had been talk of expanding federal aid to students since the post–World War II GI Bill for veterans had successfully brought thousands of students into postsecondary education, and the 1950s saw growing public concern about the "talent loss" to the nation that resulted when poor but academically talented students were not able to pursue schooling for financial reasons. Nevertheless, political conditions in that decade did not favor an increasing role for the federal government in higher education finance. Specially targeted federal aid to veterans continued after the Korean War, but proposals for more general student assistance languished.

This situation changed dramatically in 1964 and 1965. As part of the War on Poverty's broad assault on social problems, Congress and President Lyndon Johnson approved the College Work-Study Program in 1964 to subsidize employment for financially needy college students and the Educational Opportunity Grant Program for such students in 1965. (The latter is now called Supplemental Educational Opportunity Grants.) In addition, in 1965 Congress enacted the Guaranteed Student Loan Program, aimed primarily at middle-income students whose families, though not financially needy, might want help with cash-flow demands during the college years. Middle-income families had been clamoring for help with college costs; they found a responsive audience in the U.S. Senate, which almost passed a tuition-tax-credit bill in 1964. Guaranteed Student Loans were meant in part to take the steam out of efforts to pass tax-credit legislation.

Along with the previously enacted NDEA loans, a triad of federal programs (grant, loan, work) was in place by the mid-1960s; these paralleled the student aid structure created in earlier years by colleges themselves. Moreover, in 1965 Congress modified the Social Security program to allow deceased or disabled workers' children to receive educational benefits if they were enrolled in higher education, rather than ending Social Security support at the age of eighteen.

In the next few years pressures grew not only to enlarge the available aid but to make it more predictable. Students went directly to banks to obtain Guaranteed Student Loans, but the other federal aid was awarded by colleges and universities from federal appropriations. Thus, students could not know the amount of their aid, or whether they would even be eligible for assistance, until they applied to college and had been accepted. This process seemed at odds with the educational opportunity goals of the programs. In 1972, therefore, the federal government created the Basic Educational Opportunity Grant program (now called Pell Grants after Senator Claiborne Pell). These grants were meant to provide a reliable financial foundation to which each student might add assistance from various other sources, parental contributions, and funds accruing from his or her own efforts. Students would apply for the new grants directly to the federal government, and grant amounts would for the most part be determined independently of where the student ultimately enrolled. In addition to Pell Grants, the federal government created State Student Incentive Grants (SSIGs) to encourage all states to enact or expand their own grant programs. The older federal programs were left in place; student aid supporters were unwilling to count on generous funding for Pell Grants. As it happened, though, the Pell program grew quickly.

Even as these grants were phased in, however, new pressures were building. Interest in tuition tax credits for middle-income families made a reappearance. Again hoping to deflect interest in them, President Jimmy Carter and Congress approved the Middle Income Student Assistance Act in 1978. Pell Grant eligibility was expanded up the income scale, and all students, regardless of income, were made eligible for Guaranteed Student Loans.

A combination of factors led to an almost immediate backlash against the changes enacted in 1978. Unexpectedly high inflation made guaranteed loans, with their fixed 7 percent interest rate, exceedingly attractive college financing vehicles, and loan volume exploded. Federal costs associated with loan subsidies exploded as well. Then, in 1980 came the election of Ronald Reagan, who had pledged to curtail federal spending on all social programs and questioned the role of the federal government in supporting college students.

Throughout its years in office, the Reagan administration tried to scale back federal student assistance. Most of its proposals were soundly defeated by Congress, except for the phasing out of Social Security student benefits. Nevertheless, the rapid growth in federal aid that characterized the 1970s came to a halt. The purchasing power of federal student assistance actually declined for several years and only recently reached and exceeded 1980–81 levels. States and institutions picked up the pace of their spending but were unable to compensate fully for the federal losses. The eligibility changes made in 1978 were repealed, and legislation enacted at various points during the 1980s restricted guaranteed loans to only those students who could qualify on the basis of financial need. (Legislation in 1988 also changed the name of the Guaranteed Student Loan program to the Stafford Student Loan program, after Senator Robert Stafford. I shall refer to Stafford Loans throughout the remainder of this chapter.)

The only new program initiative came in the loan area. Parent Loans for Undergraduate Students (PLUS), a less-subsidized version of Stafford Loans, enabled parents to borrow regardless of income with minimal federal subsidy. Supplemental Loans for Students (SLS) expanded access to loans for certain kinds of students (graduate students and undergraduates not financially dependent on their parents), again at minimal subsidy. Income Contingent Loans (ICL) involved a very small demonstration project experimenting with new kinds of repayment schedules in the Perkins Loan program.

Despite the Reagan administration's efforts to cut back federal programs, student aid has enjoyed strong bipartisan support in Congress throughout most of its history. In recent years, however, controversies have arisen, especially over student loans, that have cast a shadow over all aid programs. One major concern has been the cost to the federal government of paying off defaulted student loans, an expense that has risen to well over $2 billion annually. Default costs have raised the specter of waste, fraud, and abuse, particularly in for-profit trade schools, which have the highest average default rates of any postsecondary sector. As these schools now account for roughly a third of Stafford Loan borrowing and well over half of SLS borrowing, problems in this sector have a major impact on student loan programs and have been a key factor tarnishing the favorable image that federal student aid enjoyed for so many years.

A Statistical Portrait of Student Aid

The current pattern of student assistance is not the result of a grand design but has evolved over the years to meet problems and perceived shortcomings. This evolution is captured in statistical terms in Table 1 and Table 2, which show aid awarded in selected years to all students (both undergraduate and graduate) in postsecondary education from all federal sources and from state and institutional grants. Table 1 indicates current dollars, and Table 2 shows dollar amounts adjusted for inflation.

These statistics demonstrate the aid available to students, *not* aid provided by program sponsors. The chief difference lies in the guaranteed

Table 1. Financial Aid Awarded to Postsecondary Students (in Millions of Current Dollars)

	1970–71	*1975–76*	*1980–81*	*1985–86*	*Preliminary 1989–90*
Federally Supported Programs					
Generally Available Aid					
Pell Grant	0	937	2,387	3,567	4,476
SEOG	134	201	368	410	442
SSIG	0	20	72	76	72
CWS	227	295	660	656	780
Perkins Loan (NDSL)	241	460	694	703	844
Income Contingent Loan			0	0	6
Guaranteed Loan	1,015	1,267	6,202	8,839	12,300
(Stafford Loans)	(1,015)	(1,267)	(6,200)	(8,328)	(9,660)
(SLS)	n/a	n/a	(0)	(269)	(1,839)
(PLUS)	n/a	n/a	(2)	(242)	(801)
Subtotal	1,617	3,180	10,383	14,251	18,920
Specially Directed Aid					
Social Security	499	1,093	1,883	0	0
Veterans	1,121	4,180	1,714	864	601
Military	64	97	201	342	366
Other Grants	16	63	122	67	112
Other Loans	42	45	62	372	350
Subtotal	1,742	5,478	3,982	1,645	1,429
Total Federal Aid	3,359	8,658	14,365	15,896	20,349
State Grant Programs	236	490	801	1,311	1,785
Institutionally Awarded Aid	965	1,435	2,060	3,674	5,728
Total Federal, State, and Institutional Aid	4,560	10,583	17,226	20,881	27,862

Source: College Board (Washington Office), 1990.

loan programs, where banks largely provide the capital and the federal government supplies support in the form of default-guaranteed and interest-rate subsidies. Nevertheless, these tables show both the emergence of the federal government as the dominant partner in the direct provision of financial aid to students and the enormous growth in the availability of student aid, reaching almost $28 billion in 1989–90.

Even though federal student aid has grown dramatically over the past three decades, postsecondary financing remains a real partnership. First, it is worth remembering that state taxpayers bear a large share of the burden of supporting colleges and students through the subsidies they provide for public institutions, which result (at least for in-state students) in tuitions that are often far below the cost of providing education. Second, nonfederal partners (states, families, and institutions) still carry much of the responsi-

Table 2. Financial Aid Awarded to Postsecondary Students (in Millions of Constant 1989 Dollars)

	1970–71	*1975–76*	*1980–81*	*1985–86*	*Preliminary 1989–90*
Federally Supported Programs					
Generally Available Aid					
Pell Grant	0	2,093	3,416	4,065	4,369
SEOG	417	449	526	467	432
SSIG	0	44	103	86	70
CWS	710	659	945	748	762
Perkins Loan (NDSL)	751	1,028	992	801	824
Income Contingent Loan					5
Guaranteed Loan	3,167	2,832	8,875	10,073	12,007
(Stafford Loans)	(3,167)	(2,832)	(8,872)	(9,490)	(9,430)
(SLS)	n/a	n/a	(0)	(306)	(1,795)
(PLUS)	n/a	n/a	(3)	(276)	(782)
Subtotal	5,045	7,105	14,857	16,240	18,469
Specially Directed Aid					
Social Security	1,557	2,443	2,694	0	0
Veterans	3,498	9,342	2,453	984	586
Military	201	216	287	390	357
Other Grants	50	141	174	77	109
Other Loans	131	101	89	424	341
Subtotal	5,437	12,243	5,697	1,875	1,393
Total Federal Aid	10,482	19,348	20,554	18,115	19,862
State Grant Programs	736	1,095	1,146	1,494	1,742
Institutionally Awarded Aid	3,011	3,207	2,948	4,187	5,592
Total Federal, State, and Institutional Aid	14,229	23,650	24,648	23,796	27,196

Source: College Board (Washington Office), 1990.

bility for meeting the out-of-pocket costs (tuitions, fees, books, and living expenses) involved in postsecondary schooling.

Data about the relative contributions of these partners to the costs of higher education in the large and diverse American system are frustratingly elusive, however. Only in 1986–87 did the federal government begin what will be a triennial survey on financing patterns, so it will be many years before we have comprehensive statistics to track changing trends. Nevertheless, data from the first National Postsecondary Student Aid Survey (NPSAS) for 1986–87 provide evidence of the contributions that the various partners make to student support.

NPSAS shows (Stowe, 1990) that among undergraduates enrolled in the fall of 1986, 49 percent received student aid from all sources, with about 35 percent reporting some federal assistance. About 40 percent of all undergraduates received grant assistance; the remaining aid recipients received help in the form of loans and/or subsidized work opportunities. A large share of higher education expenses is thus left for parents and students to pay.

Of the undergraduates who received aid, only 32 percent received support from the federal government alone. The rest received aid from a combination of federal and nonfederal sources or from nonfederal sources only. The percentage of undergraduate aid recipients who were helped by the federal government alone differed significantly by institutional sector: 15 percent in private, nonprofit colleges and universities; 33 percent in public colleges and universities; and 78 percent in private, for-profit trade schools.

Of all the financial aid received by undergraduates, about 62 percent came from federal programs—the remainder from state (11 percent), institutional (21 percent), and private (6 percent) sources. About 57 percent of aid to undergraduates was in the form of grants, with 37 percent as loans and 6 percent in the form of work-study aid. (As we shall see in the next chapter, student employment outside of formal work-study programs plays a much greater role in the student financing picture than these figures suggest.)

Assessing Need and Delivering Aid

The tradition of awarding aid to students who are financially needy goes back to prerevolutionary times, when the earliest colonial colleges made awards to the "worthy poor." Over time, however, institutionally based scholarships became in many cases a reward for the academically talented. Financially needy students might have been the original recipients, but often they had to perform well academically to keep their grants.

In the 1950s, growing college enrollments and an increasing awareness that institutional student aid resources were limited caused campus administrators to rethink the purposes of their financial aid programs. Although the idea of rewarding academic merit has never totally disappeared, both institutions and the few states with grant programs shared a growing belief that student aid should be concentrated on those individuals whose families were unable to pay for college by themselves and whose enrollment decisions were most likely to be affected by an aid award. A corollary of this belief was the principle that parents had the primary responsibility for the education of their children and should contribute to the best of their ability to meeting college expenses. As additional states and then the federal government adopted student aid programs, they built their policies upon these same two foundations: aid based on need and parental responsibility.

The recognition that student assistance should be based on financial need begs many questions, however. Is *need* just a function of what a family can afford to pay, or should it also be affected by the cost of the particular college where the student wants to enroll? Should parental ability to pay be calculated on the basis of income alone, or should other factors such as assets and extraordinary expenses be considered? How much of a family's income and/or assets should be judged available to pay for higher education? What if some families save for college and others with like incomes buy luxury goods instead and so appear more needy when the time comes to send a child to college? How can information about a family's ability to pay and financial need be collected and distributed to all the federal, state, and institutional sponsors of student aid programs without overwhelming applicants with different forms and deadlines?

The complexities of assessing financial aid need can perhaps most effectively be conveyed by making an analogy between student aid programs and a more familiar process: income taxation. Student aid, like public taxation, aims to measure a family's income and then assess a part of it. Like tax policy, student aid programs seek to make these assessments fair. This process means searching for both *horizontal equity* (treating families in like circumstances in a similar fashion) and *vertical equity* (taxing wealthier people at higher rates than poorer people on the grounds that wealthier people can better afford to pay). As with debates about taxes, discussions about student aid fairness are characterized by two fundamental dilemmas. First, though research can help determine whether various provisions help or hinder the achievement of horizontal equity, it cannot offer much assistance on issues of vertical equity. How much more to assess the wealthy than the poor (that is, what marginal tax rates should be and how progressive they should be) are matters of judgment, not fact. Second, there is an inherent contradiction between the desire to gather all the information necessary to portray a family's financial circumstances fully and accurately and the desire to keep tax/student aid forms reasonably simple and easy to complete.

This second dilemma suggests that analogies between the tax and student aid systems extend beyond assessing financial circumstances to how the data themselves are collected. Whether or not each system appears to be a simple "seamless web" to individual taxpayers or student aid applicants depends on decisions by both federal and nonfederal agents. Where taxes are concerned, federal officials have developed multiple forms to suit the financial circumstances of different taxpayers. Many states have chosen to base their own tax codes and/or forms in whole or in part on the federal model; others continue to go their own way, requiring completely different submissions from taxpayers. Sometimes state taxpayers can actually use documents from their federal tax return in their state return; in other cases they may have to provide identical data but in a format specific to the state in which they reside.

As with taxation, today's student aid policies reflect the evolution of procedures for assessing need and delivering assistance as new partners have entered and then (in the federal case) come to dominate the aid system.

The first significant effort to determine common procedures for assessing need took place at the collegiate level. In the mid-1950s a group of College Board members helped form the College Scholarship Service (CSS) as a vehicle for developing a common method that colleges could use for assessing financial need and a common financial aid application that students could submit to all CSS member schools. In the 1960s a second organization, American College Test (ACT), began providing similar services for colleges and universities. The federal government allowed institutions to use calculations of need determined in accordance with CSS and ACT methods in the awarding of funds from the new campus-based federal aid programs that were created in the late 1950s and 1960s. From its inauguration, however, the Pell Grant program had its own application and a methodology for determining eligibility that was spelled out under congressional direction by the Department of Education and subject to congressional veto.

By the mid-1970s, then, applicants for aid from federal, state, and institutional sources could find themselves completing multiple forms and having their need assessed by several different methods. The National Task Force on Student Aid Problems—a voluntary group of financial aid administrators, educational associations, students, the federal and state governments, and national need-analysis services—came together to discuss these issues and devise solutions. As a result of the task force's work, CSS and ACT agreed to merge their separate need-analysis systems into a single Uniform Methodology (UM) and to develop a common data collection form. Individual versions of the common data form might contain additional questions beyond the core that was required by nonfederal users (that is, states and institutions) for awarding their own student aid funds. The federal government continued to use its own method for calculating eligibility for Pell Grants, but it did agree to accept data collected by nonfederal servicers to determine individual student awards. Thus, though the need-analysis methods remained different, a student could apply for both federal and nonfederal aid on a single form. This process of allowing students to apply for Pell Grants through the forms they submitted to nonfederal servicers was referred to as *multiple data entry,* and the agencies involved in this system became known as multiple data entry (MDE) processors.

The 1980s have seen a continuing debate over how to assess need and who should be involved in making decisions about need-analysis methods and forms. For a number of years after the National Task Force made its recommendations, another voluntary group (the National Coalition for Coordination of Student Financial Aid) annually reviewed the Uniform Methodology and decided on modifications and updates. In 1986, however, Congress chose to write a variant of the UM (which came to be called the Congressional Methodology or CM) into law, for use in all federal aid programs except Pell and State Student Incentive Grants (a federal-state matching program). This action replaced the previous "community consensus" model for determining financial need with a federally mandated one. Because of federal rules restricting overawards of aid to students receiving federal funds, financial aid administrators found it necessary to use CM even when awarding nonfederal aid to students who also received federal assistance. Pell Grants continued to be awarded on the basis of a separate method, which also had been written into law rather than left to the Education Department to administer.

The federal government became increasingly prescriptive, too, in matters related to data collection for student aid purposes. In 1980 Congress decreed that students should be able to apply for federal funds without paying the application fee charged by the major nonfederal processors. The Department of Education enlarged what had originally been its Pell Grant application into an expanded form that included data elements it declared adequate to calculate need under the UM (later CM), as well as under the Pell need analysis method. More recently, the federal government has required that *all* forms, not just the federal application, contain a free core section by which students can be considered for federal aid.

In 1986 Congress required the Department of Education to contract with at least five MDE processors; today, six are officially recognized. Each provides individual students with a single application through which they can apply for various kinds of aid. States and institutions tell their applicants which forms they will accept and often allow any one of several. There have been almost annual changes in Department of Education rules about how MDE processors must collect the common federal data elements, about how additional information sought by many states and institutions can be integrated with the federal core, and about whether campus aid officials will be allowed to use their professional judgment (often based on additional information) to alter the financial-need figure that results from strict application of the CM or Pell need-analysis system.

From the student's point of view, the National Task Force's goal of streamlining the aid process by allowing access to multiple financial aid programs via a single application remains largely intact. (The system works better for grants than for loans, however; as Stafford Loans have become increasingly based on need, the fact that federal law requires a separate loan application has added to the paperwork required of aid applicants.) States and institutions, however, find themselves in a more complex world over which they have diminishing influence. They frequently must be prepared to receive data on large numbers of financial aid applicants from multiple sources using sophisticated electronic transmission techniques and must be able to integrate these data into a single administrative system for delivering and tracking aid at the state-agency or campus level. In this changing world of aid administration, questions about how state and campus requirements can be accommodated within an increasingly federal-oriented system and about how to finance processing and record-keeping services beyond those provided under federal MDE contracts remain to be resolved.

Policy Issues for the 1990s

The world of the 1990s, both politically and economically, is likely to be quite different from the world of the 1960s, 1970s, and 1980s, in which federal student aid programs were born and grew to maturity. The major policy issues that will be debated in the years ahead will be discussed against a backdrop of budget stringency caused by the necessity of bringing spiralling federal deficits under control and in the face of the first economic downturn in a decade. Such conditions will not only affect the federal government but will strain states, institutions, and families as well. Given the preeminent role Washington now plays in the student aid arena, how federal policymakers sort out the following issues of priorities and trade-offs will significantly affect all of the partners who are part of the complex mosaic of the American postsecondary financing system.

Federal Aid's Goals and Beneficiaries. One consequence of the evolutionary development of federal student aid is that its goals and intended beneficiaries are murky. In the 1980s the Reagan administration challenged federal assistance programs on the grounds that they had not equalized educational opportunity and that they often benefited institutions rather than students. Does the failure to make much progress toward equalizing opportunity mean that federal programs have also failed? Is it bad if aid to students helps institutions as well? Is aid reaching the students and institutions that federal policymakers think it should?

McPherson (1988) has suggested an analytical framework for assessing student aid that can help answer these questions. Based on both explicit program objectives and the legislative record of their enactment, he argues that federal student aid has three major purposes: equalizing educational opportunity, making the sharing of higher education's costs and benefits fairer, and helping higher education institutions work better by making them financially more secure.

Equalizing opportunity was the explicit rationale for the creation of most federal student aid. Yet it is an objective difficult to measure and even more difficult to achieve. An important realization has resulted from recent scrutiny of aid programs: they are not sufficient by themselves to reach traditionally underserved populations. Too many students are lost well before college becomes a real possibility. They either drop out of school altogether or make academic choices that leave them educationally unprepared for higher education. Increasing interest is being expressed in "early intervention" programs aimed at junior high and even elementary school students and in programs like New York State's recently enacted Liberty Scholarships, which offer guarantees of financial support for college many years in advance.

Despite student aid's limitations, however, research does suggest that educational opportunity is more equal than it would have been without these programs. In a world of limited resources, the benefits of expanding federal programs to include early intervention activities will have to be balanced against the effects on student aid if these are funded at the expense of student assistance programs.

McPherson's framework also reminds us that the success of student aid cannot be measured exclusively by the extent to which it equalizes access to education. Greater fairness in the distribution of costs and benefits might be achieved among those students who do enroll even if the record of expanding opportunity to underserved groups is mixed. Institutional effectiveness might be enhanced by federal support, but that support might be most efficiently given through a market mechanism: that is, through students choosing which school to attend. In fact, the legislative debates that took place in Congress in 1972 over the provision of institutional or student aid—debates that resulted in the creation of Pell Grants—indicated that institutional support was indeed seen as a legitimate byproduct of student aid.

Many of the questions that characterize current student aid debates grow out of concerns over fairness and institutional support. For example, does fairness mean targeting aid on students with the lowest incomes or the greatest need? Middle-income students may have comparatively high need if they attend high-cost institutions. The rhetoric of federal student aid has emphasized its role in providing both *access* to higher education and *choice* among different kinds of institutions. However, the biggest federal grant program, Pell Grants, no longer serves middle-income students and has become almost completely insensitive to cost differences among institutions because maximum grant levels have grown very slowly. Both middle-income families and private nonprofit colleges increasingly feel excluded. Many middle-income families have also seen their eligibility for subsidized student loans diminish or disappear as income restrictions have been reimposed and tightened. Meanwhile, increasing proportions of federal student aid funds are going to students in proprietary trade schools—about a quarter of Pell Grants and, as noted above, sizable amounts of Stafford and SLS loans.

Growing student diversity results in additional groups whose access to federal aid has been limited and who now desire inclusion. Congress responded to emerging concerns about less-than-half-time students (many of whom are among the sizable number of older students now enrolling in college) when it made such students eligible for Pell Grants in 1986. Because of budget limitations, though, such students only received Pell Grants for one year and have subsequently been made ineligible again.

With resources limited, student aid debates in the 1990s will increasingly be about which students and schools student aid should be intended to serve.

Program Structure and Balance. Closely related to questions about the goals of federal student aid are issues of program structure and balance. Pell Grants and Stafford Student Loans have emerged as the two major federal programs aiding undergraduates. Much concern has been expressed about the balance of grant and loan funding and about whether too much emphasis is being placed on borrowing. This topic will be explored in the next chapter on the role of students and parents in meeting postsecondary expenses.

The growth of student loan programs has also drawn attention to several structural issues that are the subject of some controversy. Federal dollars spent on these programs have a powerful leveraging effect because of the far greater amounts of money they generate in student loans from private capital markets. Banks are the primary lenders in the guaranteed loan programs. State-designated guarantee agencies insure the loans against default and in turn receive reinsurance from the federal government. Washington also pays the interest on student loans while the borrower remains in college and subsidizes the interest rate (through a so-called special allowance to lenders) as long as the loan is in repayment. The special allowance keeps the interest charge to the student borrower at below-market rates while providing the competitive returns banks demand to remain in the program. Yet two aspects of this arrangement have proved problematic: the subsidies and the reliance on private capital markets.

Stafford Loans actually contain three types of subsidy: the guarantee against default; the in-college interest payment; and the special allowance. The default guarantee is generally believed to be essential to a program that relies on private capital markets, as students borrowing to pay for education are not obtaining a tangible asset that can be repossessed in case of nonpayment. The cost of this guarantee has become controversial as defaults have risen, and there is talk of reducing the banks' insurance from 100 percent to something less to encourage due diligence in loan collection. But there seems to be no feasible alternative to the guarantee at some substantial level. Similarly pragmatic reasons favor the in-college subsidy. A financially needy student presumably does not have the resources to pay interest or interest-and-principal until he or she finishes or leaves college and enters the work force.

The really troublesome subsidy is the special allowance. It makes the Stafford Loan program extremely volatile in terms of federal costs and therefore makes the whole program politically vulnerable when interest rates in the economy rise. Borrowers pay a fixed interest rate: 8 percent in the first four years of repayment and 10 percent thereafter. Lenders receive a total return equal to the 91-day Treasury bill rate plus 3¼ percent. The difference between the total return and the rate charged to borrowers is the special allowance rate. When interest in the economy skyrocketed in the early 1980s, so did the special allowance, and therefore Stafford Loan, costs. Although concern about this problem has abated as interest rates have fallen, it remains an even more dangerous threat as the federal government tries to bring spending under control. The danger is that an unexpected surge in mandatory spending for Stafford Loan subsidies will threaten federal funding for grant programs.

In a time of fiscal austerity, the fact that the federal government subsidizes borrowing through the special allowance also forces it to limit who can borrow in ways that may not be desirable. If the idea that student borrowing represents an investment in the nation's own future has merit, then it makes sense for all students to have access to loans, not just those whose family circumstances now cause them to qualify as financially needy. The abortive experience with the Middle Income Student Assistance Act of 1978 made it clear that we cannot afford to give all comers access to subsidized loans, however. It is therefore necessary to limit borrowing because the Stafford Student Loan Program mixes loans (which theoretically are logical for all students) with subsidies (which must be restricted to the financially needy).

Finally, the use of private markets rather than government credit to provide loan capital is both helpful and problematic. On the one hand, financial institutions have provided convenient access to billions of loan dollars annually, and secondary markets have evolved as efficient and sometimes innovative intermediaries between lending institutions and worldwide capital markets. But on the other hand, these accomplishments may come at a cost to the taxpayers. Stafford Loan critics argue that the program provides banks with a riskless and extremely profitable product; lenders claim that student loans are expensive to administer (particularly due to growing regulation) and offer narrow profit margins. Despite the elaborate private market structure, in fact, no market mechanism is operating. As both interest rates to borrowers and returns to lenders are fixed, there is no way to capture the presumed efficiencies of a marketplace. In addition, the true costs of the programs have been hidden because of a failure to record future government liabilities incurred when loan commitments are made—although recently enacted federal credit reform policies will change this practice. Finally, heavy marketing of Stafford Loans by competing banks may encourage students to take on more debt than they otherwise would.

Accountability and Performance. In the 1950s and 1960s, when federal aid to education was still one of the nation's most controversial issues, opponents argued that federal funding was sure to be followed by federal regulation. Bankers have been complaining for years about perceived overregulation in the student loan program. Postsecondary institutions as well are increasingly concerned about the regulations and paperwork accompanying federal student aid. The impulse to regulate stems from several sources: efforts to insure proper program administration, congressional desire to use federal student aid as a lever to foster compliance with other federal goals, and a growing emphasis on accountability and performance standards as a way to counter perceived abuses (especially abuses that appear to increase student loan default rates) in institutions where student aid recipients enroll.

Regulation to insure that federal funds are awarded to eligible students in the proper amounts is the least controversial, though it can result in significant paperwork requirements at the campus level. Perhaps less noticeable to administrators outside the aid office is the extent to which federal student aid has been made the tool of other federal purposes. Applicants must pledge that they are in compliance with Selective Service laws about draft registration and that they do not use drugs. Schools whose students receive federal aid become subject to federal civil rights laws, to drug abuse prevention laws, and to recent legislation on campus security. A new law also calls on institutions that receive federal aid to report on graduation rates of full-time, degree-seeking students, a measure initially prompted by concerns over exploitation of student athletes.

This latter measure moves the federal government closer to issues of educational purpose and performance than has historically been true, and this trend is likely to continue as Congress seeks ways to counter abuses that have become apparent particularly in connection with student loans. Though federal officials acknowledge that they are currently prohibited from directly assessing the quality of educational programs, they talk of strengthening state licensing, accreditation, and certification standards and of establishing performance measures like retention and graduation rates (the latter by program), job-placement figures, and others as ways to insure that students receiving federal funds are not being taken advantage of. There appears to be a reluctance to regulate "selectively" (that is, with regulations focussed on problem schools, such as those with high default rates), though some of the Department of Education's 1990 default-reduction initiatives did make such distinctions. All postsecondary institutions, therefore, face the prospect of closer federal scrutiny of their activities, and across a broader front, than ever before.

Simplification. Our system of student aid, if one can call it a system, is admittedly complex. The multiplicity of programs and sponsors reflects our federal structure and decentralized responsibility for providing and financing postsecondary education. I noted earlier the efforts that were made beginning in the mid-1970s to unify need assessment and aid delivery. Even though most students are faced with only one financial aid application to complete, applications appear to many observers to be overly complicated, and separate need-assessment systems remain for Pell Grants and the other federal programs.

A major issue during the upcoming reauthorization of the Higher Education Act (scheduled for completion by September 30, 1992) is simplification of the student aid delivery system. Efforts to simplify are likely to focus on designing a single need-analysis system for all federal programs and reducing the amount of information collected from parents and students. These two elements are interconnected, of course, because the degree of discrimination that the need-analysis system can make between families in different financial circumstances depends on how much and what kind of information is collected.

Some observers have argued that need assessment for the major federal programs, Pell Grants and Stafford Loans, could be far less detailed than it is now. To achieve the equity/simplicity trade-off that was described earlier in this chapter, it might be adequate for federal programs to settle for "rough justice" and for the need-analysis system to produce just a "good enough" number, rather than a finely tuned index, of financial circumstances. As the foundation of the financial aid system, Pell Grants are fairly narrowly targeted on lower income students and, as we saw earlier, are not particularly sensitive to college costs. Stafford Loans, though rather heavily subsidized, represent an effort on the part of students to help themselves by incurring a repayable obligation. In both cases, it might be reasonable to conclude that federal purposes would be well served by making applications and need assessment far simpler, even though some degree of equity might be sacrificed in the bargain.

Two considerations need to be kept in mind as such a trade-off is contemplated, however. First, to the extent that changes are made to open federal programs to students from families further up the income scale (for example, to help middle-income students), the trade-off between equity and simplicity becomes larger. Wealthier families have income and assets that are more complicated to measure than do families whose financial capacity can be quite adequately captured by looking at their wage or salary income alone.

Second, nonfederal providers of aid may not have the same reasons to accept rough justice or pretty good numbers that federal policymakers do. States and institutions award mostly grants, not loans, and frequently find middle-income students eligible for their programs. Institutional officials, who build their aid packages on top of state and federal assistance, especially must determine (as their federal counterparts need not) how much remaining need exists when costs and other aid are considered. This process often means dealing precisely with the kinds of families who are not eligible for federal programs and whose financial circumstances cannot be captured simply. Yet in a federally driven system, it is not clear that moves toward simplification, when coupled with overaward rules, will allow sufficient flexibility for these other aid providers to make their own decisions about the equity/simplicity trade-off.

References

College Board (Washington Office). *Trends in Student Aid: 1980 to 1990.* New York: College Board, 1990.

Johnstone, D. B. *Sharing the Costs of Higher Education: Student Financial Assistance in the United Kingdom, the Federal Republic of Germany, France, Sweden, and the United States.* New York: College Board, 1986.

McPherson, M. S. *How Can We Tell If Federal Student Aid Is Working?* New York: College Board, 1988.

Stowe, P. *Undergraduate Financial Aid Awards: A Report of the 1987 National Postsecondary Student Aid Study.* Washington, D.C.: U.S. Department of Education, National Center for Education Statistics, 1990.

Janet S. Hansen is director for policy analysis in the Washington, D.C., office of the College Board.

The 1980s saw a renewed emphasis on parental and student responsibility for financing higher education, as federal aid programs and family incomes lagged behind college costs.

The Shifting Roles of Parents and Students

Janet S. Hansen

Chapter One demonstrates that the division of responsibility for financing postsecondary education is not static but has changed over time. Sometimes these shifts have resulted from explicit policy decisions, as when states and the federal government have chosen to expand their roles in providing student aid. Especially in recent years, the shifts have occurred more as a result of general economic and fiscal pressures rather than a strong desire on the part of policymakers to alter the balance of responsibility for meeting college costs.

Nevertheless, the balance does appear to have altered, with parents and students bearing more of the burden than they did in the 1970s. This change has focused attention on the financing mechanisms available to families, raising questions about whether students are carrying too much of the load (especially through borrowing) and spurring interest in new investment vehicles to help parents meet their traditional obligations.

The Shifting Burden of Paying for College

The gradual development of the federal student aid structure that began in the late 1950s reached maturity in 1972 with the creation of the capstone Pell Grant program. In the next few years, federal assistance flourished. Assistance from Department of Education grant programs grew twentyfold between 1970-71 and 1980-81. Even after adjusting for inflation, grant aid from this source grew nearly tenfold. At the same time, sizable amounts of assistance were provided to students through the Social Security and veterans' programs, assistance whose buying power after adjusting for inflation remained about constant over the decade. With the costs of attending college actually trailing inflation, the burden of paying for postsecondary education appeared to be shifting from families to federal taxpayers. Moreover, taxpayers also subsidized a growing volume of student loans, further easing the problem of paying postsecondary expenses.

The picture became significantly more complicated in the 1980s. The growth in Department of Education grants slowed at the same time that college costs grew dramatically. Social Security student benefits were eliminated, and veterans benefits declined as Vietnam-era veterans exhausted their eligibility. Loan volume continued to grow. State and institutional grants also increased but did not fully compensate for changes in grant assistance at the federal level. Between 1980–81 and 1989–90, the two largest federal programs aiding undergraduates (Pell Grants and guaranteed loans) grew by roughly 85 percent, whereas cost increases in public and private four-year colleges and universities went up from 100 to 134 percent. These facts together suggested that the burden of postsecondary expenses was shifting back toward families, especially students.

Families expressed growing alarm in the 1980s about their ability to pay for postsecondary education. This alarm was partially a reflection of the student aid and college-cost trends already described. But it reflected another economic reality as well. A major change took place in American income patterns around 1973. Until then, the prosperity that characterized the country had resulted in a rising economic tide that made everyone better off in absolute terms, even if it did not change relative income levels much. Regardless of where they stood in the statistical income distribution, more and more people felt themselves able to purchase what we think of as elements of a middle-class life-style: houses, cars, and many other consumer goods, as well as college educations for their children. But during the mid-1970s, the rapid income growth that had characterized virtually all sectors of American society in the post–World War II era came to a halt. Median-family-income growth, after adjusting for inflation, stagnated. This has led to a phenomenon economist Frank Levy (1989) has described as "the vanishing middle class," whose middle-class life-style has also been disappearing.

In the case of college, reaction to these economic realities may have been delayed by several factors. College charges grew roughly in tandem with incomes in the 1970s; only in the 1980s did they routinely outstrip family income growth. Moreover, disparities between income growth and college costs were different at different income levels. Though all families were affected by the slowdown of the 1970s, only the wealthiest fifth of families saw their real incomes rising in the 1980s; the others continued to see little growth. For a while, families could insulate themselves against the effects of stagnant salaries and wages by borrowing more, saving less, and sending additional family members into the work force, all of which happened in the years after 1973. But such compensating steps have their limits, and families who felt their ability to sustain a middle-class life-style threatened were increasingly heard pleading for help with college costs in the 1980s.

One final comment is relevant to this discussion: fewer and fewer members of an increasingly diverse student population have parents who can be expected to help them pay for college, though the traditional model of financing has assumed parental support. In the fall of 1986, 40 percent of all undergraduates were twenty-four years of age or older. Only 63 percent of all undergraduates were financially dependent on their parents. These changes in the student body have been reflected in student aid programs. The percentage of Pell Grants going to financially independent students was about 58 percent in 1988–89.

Student Loans: Overburdening a Generation?

One of the most persistent concerns of the past decade has been that students are becoming too heavily mortgaged by the debt they incur to finance their postsecondary education. These fears were fueled by tremendous and largely unplanned growth in student loan programs. Annual Stafford Loan volume increased from a modest $1.3 billion in the mid-1970s to an estimated $9.7 billion in 1989–90. Supplemental Student Loans, only $15 million in 1981–82 (when they went by the name Auxiliary Loans to Assist Students), skyrocketed to an estimated $1.8 billion in 1989–90. Rising student defaults (briefly discussed in Chapter One) have drawn further attention to the issue.

Much of the growth in student loans had already taken place when the Joint Economic Committee of the Congress commissioned me in 1986 to examine whether student loans were overburdening a generation. The resulting report (Hansen, 1987) identified a problem that persists to this day: the paucity of data with which to assess concerns about overborrowing. The report noted that "data and studies on the impact of student borrowing are few, fragmentary, and frequently out-of-date and/or contradictory." It pointed to a "pressing need for better data and research on student borrowing to help separate valid from invalid concerns about high borrowing levels."

After surveying the existing information, the study concluded that the most frequently heard concerns were not supported by the evidence. High debt levels were relatively rare and did not appear to be causing serious problems for many students; nor were educational, career, or personal decisions apparently affected by indebtedness. Defaults, although a growing problem, were not typically found among students with high debt levels. Instead, defaulters tended to be students who had borrowed only once or twice, who had relatively low levels of debt, who stayed in school for a short time, and who failed to obtain a degree or certificate. Such students were to be found disproportionately in proprietary schools; consequently, the default rate among proprietary institutions far exceeded that in other sectors of postsecondary education.

Based on the fragmentary evidence available at the time, the study concluded that, though the incidence of borrowing had clearly increased, fewer than half of all students appeared to borrow at some time while they were enrolled. There were significant differences among borrowers of various types (graduate students versus undergraduates, full-timers versus part-timers, private, nonprofit school students versus those enrolled in public or proprietary institutions). Borrowers came from a wide range of economic circumstances. Once regarded as primarily for the middle class, student loans had become an important financing vehicle for students from lower-income families as well.

Data from the first National Postsecondary Student Aid Study (NPSAS) subsequently confirmed these impressions about student borrowing. According to our analyses of NPSAS data, about 24 percent of all undergraduates enrolled in the fall of 1986 borrowed at some point during academic year 1986–87. The vast majority of all borrowing was done through the federal student loan programs. The proportion of undergraduates assuming debt varied enormously among sectors, from 70 percent in proprietary schools to 8 percent in two-year public colleges. At four-year public institutions 26 percent of undergraduates borrowed; the figure was 40 percent at private colleges and universities. The proportion of full-time undergraduates who borrowed was higher, but not dramatically so, in the traditional collegiate sectors. In proprietary schools full-time students actually borrowed at a somewhat lower rate than did all proprietary students.

The amounts that students borrowed were quite variable as well. About 50 percent of students in public two-year colleges who took out loans borrowed less than $2,000 in 1986–87. On the other hand, over 80 percent of proprietary-school borrowers took out loans of more than $2,000; the comparable figure at private colleges and universities was about 75 percent.

Cumulative debt levels naturally rose the longer students stayed in school. Among seniors, those enrolled in four-year doctoral institutions had cumulative debts averaging $6,223, whereas those at other four-year public schools had debts averaging $5,697. Debt levels among seniors at private, nonprofit institutions reflected the higher costs in that sector: an average of $10,387 at four-year doctoral universities and $8,406 at other four-year colleges.

Although the amount lent to students under federal loan programs rose about 30 percent between 1986–87 and 1989–90, numerous alterations to the programs have made it difficult to assess changes in borrowing patterns among undergraduate students. A complete picture awaits the release of the full data set from the second NPSAS study, covering academic year 1989-90, which will become available sometime in 1991. Until then, we continue to rely on fragmentary evidence to assess the impact of student borrowing.

It appears, however, that at least among financially dependent undergraduates, borrowing may have leveled off or declined in the past few years. This change is largely the result of modifications in Stafford Student Loans that have restricted eligibility. In 1986-87 any undergraduate whose family income was less than $30,000 qualified automatically for a maximum Stafford Loan. Families above this income level were eligible only if they could show financial need, but need could be calculated by a formula that excluded parental assets from consideration. After 1986-87 all Stafford Loan eligibility was based on need, and need analysis included a review of parental assets.

Furthermore, the introduction of the Congressional Methodology (CM) (see Chapters One and Four) for academic year 1988-89 further reduced eligibility for Stafford Loans by reducing calculated need. Compared to the method it replaced, CM substantially increased the contribution expected from families of dependent students. At the same time, CM greatly increased calculated need, and therefore eligibility for financial aid, for financially independent students, especially those with dependents.

Even though the 1986 reauthorization of the Higher Education Act increased maximum Stafford Loans for juniors and seniors (as well as for graduate students), it appears that the net result of all the changes has been to reduce loan eligibility among dependent undergraduates. Several states have reported large declines in the number of borrowers at public colleges (where costs are lower and many students therefore show no financial need). Eligibility even at private colleges, especially among families that consider themselves middle class, has been reduced because of the imposition of the more stringent need analysis.

Borrowing increases since 1986-87 are more likely to be found among financially independent students, especially those with dependents of their own. As many of these students have relatively low incomes (in part because they are students, not full-time workers), their growing representation among student borrowers may be contributing to the emerging perception that borrowing is increasing among low-income students. In fact, data from at least one state (New Jersey) indicate that the number of low-income dependent students who borrow has declined. It will be important to sort out these varied patterns as better data become available in order to make informed policy choices about appropriate levels of student indebtedness.

As noted previously, the growing importance of loans in the array of financial assistance options available to students has raised concerns about overreliance on debt and about the need for more emphasis on student grant and work programs. Researchers have never been able to agree on what level of debt is likely to be manageable for those who borrow to pay for college; given this lack of consensus, it becomes difficult for policymakers to know if and when the point of "too much" borrowing is reached. Better information on student debt levels and on borrowers' subsequent earnings and repayment experience will continue to be important in monitoring the effects of student loan programs. This monitoring will take on increased importance if conditions in the national economy worsen, because debt that is entirely manageable in times of high employment and real-income growth can become quite burdensome when unemployment grows and debtors find their paychecks falling behind the cost of living.

Student Employment

Today's students contribute to their educations by borrowing to a far greater degree than did their parents; they also contribute by working at paying jobs while in school. In this, they may not be so unlike their elders; Axt (1952) observed that the boast, " 'I worked my way through college' has been a part of the traditional success story of the self-made man." In fact, although student borrowing has been the focus of much policy debate over the past decade, student employment is actually much more common and also appears to have been growing. The educational implications of these facts remain largely unexplored.

A recent American Council on Education report (Hexter, 1990), based on data issued by the Bureau of Labor Statistics, found that 62 percent of all students were working in the fall of 1988. Among traditional-age (age sixteen to twenty-four), full-time students, the percentage was 47 percent, up from 35 percent in 1972. Older and/or part-time students worked at even higher rates. Full-time students worked an average of twenty hours per week, with one of five working thirty hours or more and one in ten working thirty-five or more hours, the equivalent of a full-time job. The employment rate varied among institutional sectors (with 68 percent of sixteen- to twenty-four-year-olds at two-year institutions working, compared to 48 percent of such students at four-year colleges).

These statistics are remarkably similar to the findings for fall 1986 undergraduates from the first NPSAS study. The greater detail to be found in NPSAS allows some additional observations about student employment patterns.

According to NPSAS, 61 percent of the undergraduates enrolled in the fall of 1986 were employed during the fall academic term. Though employment rates varied among institutional sectors and income groups, the similarities (especially for students from families of different income levels) are more remarkable than the differences. More than 40 percent of students in four-year public and private colleges whose family incomes exceeded $50,000 had jobs, compared to just over half of the poorest students in those institutions. Two-thirds to three-fourths of community college students at all income levels worked. Financially independent students were more likely than dependent students to work at four-year public and private colleges, though not at two-year public and proprietary schools.

Institutional sector defines sharper differences where the *amount* of work is concerned. Over 60 percent of employed full-time students at four-year public and private colleges worked twenty hours per week or fewer, whereas about 60 percent of two-year public and proprietary employed students worked more than twenty hours.

Students can contribute to their educational expenses by either working or borrowing or both; NPSAS suggests that the situation in academic year 1986–87 may have allowed students an important element of choice in deciding which they preferred. (Loan eligibility was still comparatively liberal; the restrictions described above had not yet been imposed.) Only about 13 percent of all undergraduates enrolled in the fall of 1986 reported *both* working and borrowing. This ranged from a low of 4 percent at two-year public colleges to 36 percent at proprietary schools. (The figures at four-year public and private colleges were 13 percent and 22 percent respectively.) The pattern among full-time students was roughly comparable. In two- and four-year colleges, approximately a third of all full-time students neither worked nor borrowed.

The prevalence of student employment, whether or not accompanied by borrowing, raises some important educational questions, as the American Council on Education report noted. Students appear to be taking longer to complete academic programs. Can this fact be linked to the growth in employment? It is also unclear what effect the growing importance of work has on campus life. Working students may not have time to participate in campus activities and may give less out-of-class attention to their studies. Public policy, too, must take into account the amount of time students already spend in employment. For example, proposals like the ones for required community service that received much attention in Washington in 1989 and 1990 largely ignored the fact that the majority of students are already spending substantial amounts of time working in addition to their studies and failed to address how such students would be affected by an additional service requirement.

The Role of Parents: College Savings Plans

Increases in student borrowing and employment, along with a mounting public outcry about college costs and the affordability of higher education, have led to a widespread perception that parents are less willing than previously to pay for college. This perception is difficult to document, however, and in fact surveys like NPSAS suggest that most dependent students still do rely on their families to help meet postsecondary expenses.

Nevertheless, rising college costs and stagnating family incomes have made college affordability a major public issue. At the same time, mounting federal and state budget deficits limit the possibility that large additional subsidies will be available to help college students. This situation, which suggests that parents will continue to play a crucial role in college financing, has stimulated both state and federal efforts to encourage financially able parents to plan and save for college costs.

Something of a political fire storm was ignited in 1986 when the state of Michigan enacted an innovative scheme called the Michigan Education Trust (MET). Under MET, state residents could purchase contracts guaranteed to cover tuition at any of the state's public colleges and universities at some specified time in the future. Various provisions were included to cover the possibility that the child who was the designated beneficiary might choose to enroll at a private or out-of-state institution or might not enroll in college at all. Though created by the state and housed in the Treasury Department, MET was not a state agency, and its financial obligations were not backed up by a full faith-and-credit guarantee from the state.

The novel idea of prepaying tuition, and thus removing the uncertainty about whether college would be affordable at some future point, had immediate and widespread appeal. Bills to create or study similar plans were introduced in almost every state legislature in the year or two following Michigan's action. By late 1990 thirteen states had enacted some kind of guaranteed tuition plan, and five states had operational programs.

MET has been dogged by controversy, however, and some of the states that originally passed guaranteed tuition plans later had second thoughts and changed or failed to implement them. Questions have been raised about the prices set for tuition contracts in Michigan and about the actuarial assumptions on which they were based. If initial prices are too low and/or investment returns fail to achieve planned levels, the trust could eventually have difficulty meeting its obligations. The result could be either public pressure to hold public tuition levels down artificially or the plan's bankruptcy. In the very first year of the program, Governor James Blanchard exerted strong pressure on public universities to hold their tuition increases below previously planned levels, a step that was widely regarded as MET-related. The program is also perceived as disproportionately serving wealthier families, contrary to initial promises.

MET's biggest headache, however, has come from the Internal Revenue Service. In a private letter ruling, which the state is appealing, IRS ruled that MET does not enjoy the tax exemption of a state agency and must pay income taxes on its earnings. In addition, student beneficiaries incur tax liabilities on the differences between the price of tuition contracts and their value when redeemed. These tax consequences remove most if not all of the financial advantage that a family might gain by participating in MET rather than saving for college through some other investment vehicle.

Other states have managed to avoid some of the pitfalls of MET through different financial and administrative arrangements. Nevertheless, uncertainties over the wisdom of committing future governments to unknown fiscal obligations (and in some states legal strictures against doing so) deterred many states from following Michigan's lead.

A number have opted instead to develop college savings plans that rely on an existing, tax-advantaged financial vehicle: state tax-exempt bonds. States already have the authority to issue general obligation or revenue bonds (typically to fund construction of public buildings, roads, bridges, and so on) that are exempt from federal and state taxation. Such bonds are usually issued in fairly high denominations and traditionally have appealed largely to wealthy individuals or institutional investors. To make these bonds attractive to smaller investors as a means of accruing college savings, state agencies restructure all or part of a planned bond issue. College savings bonds are usually zero-coupon bonds with comparatively low face values. They are sold at deep discounts, with interest paid only at maturity. The combination of low face values and zero-coupon structure keeps the price to purchasers within the financial reach of low- and middle-income households.

At the end of 1990, twenty-four states had operational college savings bond programs. Compared to guaranteed tuition plans, college savings bond programs have been relatively noncontroversial. They pose no risk to states in unknown future financial liabilities (though they do add to the level of state indebtedness because neither principal nor interest is paid until maturity). As they are backed by the full faith-and-credit of the state, they are safe, conservative investments for savers, and they give purchasers flexibility since their use is not restricted to college expenses. They may not always be available when savers want them, however, as some states have offered a college savings bond issue only once or infrequently. Moreover, the rate of return is not guaranteed to match the increase in college costs, so families who buy college savings bonds still face some uncertainty about the future affordability of higher education. Nevertheless, the bonds have been very popular in every state where they have been sold.

The federal government, too, has created a savings vehicle for college, in Washington's case an offshoot of familiar U.S. Series EE Savings Bonds. Parents who purchase Series EE Bonds on or after January 1, 1990, and who later use them to meet designated college expenses will not be subject to federal income tax on the proceeds. U.S. Savings Bonds are already exempt from state and local taxes. Eligible expenses include tuition and required fees; room and board payments are not covered. Eligible expenses must be calculated net of scholarships, fellowships, and other reductions in tuition.

How popular and effective U.S. Savings Bonds will be as a college savings vehicle is unclear. Such bonds have historically been a favorite of the relatively small saver; they are easy to purchase, they are safe, and they come in small denominations. Prices are also low because the issue price is only one-half of the bond's face value. Interest builds up and is paid when the bond is redeemed.

Nevertheless, families may have a difficult time calculating whether they will be eligible for the federal tax exemption that is the key feature in making U.S. Savings Bonds desirable. To keep down federal costs, Congress restricted full eligibility for federal tax exemption to families whose incomes are below specified levels ($60,000 in adjusted gross income, with modifications, in 1990 dollars for married couples). Eligibility is phased out above these levels until it disappears entirely (for example, at $90,000 for married couples). These income restrictions come into play at the time the bond is redeemed, not when it is purchased. Calculating eligibility for the tax exemption will be further complicated by the requirement that eligible expenses be reduced by the amounts of scholarships and fellowships.

Despite the shortcomings noted in all these college savings plans, however, they mark an important new development in the American system of financing postsecondary education. Paying for college is one of life's major financial undertakings for most families (along with purchasing homes and providing for retirement). Yet until recently the need to help families prepare for this event received comparatively little public attention. As a result of state and federal actions of the past four years, parents have far more information about the importance of saving for college and a wider choice of ways in which to do so than ever before. The new plans reaffirm the central role of parents in the college financing partnership and should help insure that parents continue to play this role in the future.

Conclusion

Keeping college affordable will be ever more challenging in the 1990s. Changing demographic patterns indicate that the population of potential collegegoers will be increasingly diverse, both ethnically and socioeconomically. Fewer and fewer students, even those of traditional college age, will have parents who can afford to pay for postsecondary schooling without help. Fiscal conditions in both the states and in Washington suggest that additional public subsidies may be difficult to find for the foreseeable future.

Such conditions underline the importance both of giving explicit attention to how much financial responsibility for higher education should fall to parents and students and of insuring that appropriate mechanisms are in place to help them meet these responsibilities. The shifting burdens of the past decade came about largely without design. The risk of continuing business as usual in this regard is that important segments of the American population may find access to postsecondary schooling more difficult even as the nation's need for highly educated manpower grows greater.

References

Axt, R. G. *The Federal Government and Financing Higher Education.* New York: Columbia University Press for the Commission on Financing Higher Education, 1952.
Hansen, J. S. *Student Loans: Are They Overburdening a Generation?* New York: College Board, 1987.
Hexter, H. *Students Who Work: A Profile.* American Council on Education Research Briefs, vol. 1, no. 2. Washington, D.C.: American Council on Education, 1990.
Levy, F. "Paying for College: A New Look at Family Income Trends." *College Board Review,* 1989, *182,* 18–21.

Janet S. Hansen is director for policy analysis in the Washington, D.C., office of the College Board.

A strengthened student aid partnership needs to use existing funds more efficiently, regulate how students receive aid more effectively, and delineate the rights and responsibilities of each of the major partners more adequately.

Strengthening and Refining the Federal-State-Institutional Partnership

Jamie P. Merisotis

Much has been written and spoken about the federal role in improving the prospects of equal educational opportunity for all students. This focus on the federal government has occurred primarily because its commitment to student aid programs, which now totals more than $20 billion, is the central means through which access to higher education is achieved. In direct aid to students, the federal government accounts for about three-quarters of all aid awarded.

Though the federal financial commitment is clearly the largest, there has been a widening gulf between appearance and reality with respect to the other providers and regulators of student aid. That is to say, because the federal commitment to student aid is now so large—at least relative to the commitment of two decades ago—the role of the other participants in the student aid game is dwarfed. However, both the states (and several agencies within each state) and institutions have a crucial part to play. Their contributions are both complementary to, and in some cases better suited to student needs than, the contributions of the federal government.

For example, in actual dollars the federal government awarded about $5 billion in need-based grants to students in 1989-90. The vast majority of the remaining federal awards came in the form of need-based loans, to the tune of about $13 billion in 1989-90. By comparison, states and institutions provide relatively little in loan support to students (exact figures are not available) but do offer significant funding in terms of grants. In 1989-90 the states provided approximately $1.6 billion in direct grants to students. In that same year, higher education institutions supplied nearly $6 billion in student grant aid. Thus, the combined state and institutional contribution to the fundamental means of ensuring access—grants—exceeded that of the federal government by more than $2 billion.

Overreliance by needy students on federal support is a problem that could become acute over the next several years. This problem may occur not only because of the major emphasis placed on loans, but also because of tight budgetary constraints placed on federal spending. Through the Budget Enforcement Act of 1990, the ability of the federal government to expand greatly its commitments to student aid, especially to large, new programs, will likely be hampered. In fact, the Budget Enforcement Act limits spending over a five-year period and, barring a major positive economic change, will be the most important factor that student aid advocates will have to contend with. This budget ceiling is a significant shortcoming that must be recognized and dealt with now in anticipation of tighter fiscal times over the next several years.

At the same time, there is a growing sense that existing student aid funds—from both federal and other sources—need to be more efficiently utilized. The rapidly growing dollar amount of student loan defaults, the increasing absorption of existing student aid monies by for-profit vocational (proprietary) schools, the lack of adequate "leveraging" mechanisms to stimulate new investment in student aid by states and institutions—these and other factors all point to the necessity for a greatly improved partnership in student aid. This partnership must use existing funds more efficiently, regulate how students receive that aid more effectively, and delineate the rights and responsibilities of each of the major players involved in student aid more adequately.

There are several areas in which the federal government, states, and institutions could cooperate and coordinate their efforts. A strengthened approach to student aid, with each of the partners in the process understanding clearly what its rights and commitments are, would benefit taxpayers, institutions, and, perhaps most important of all, the students for whom aid programs are designed. Several means for strengthening and refining this partnership are available. Examples of these are described below.

New Approaches to "Incentive" Funding

Perhaps the most explicit way in which the two governmental partners currently cooperate is through the State Student Incentive Grant (SSIG) program, the only direct partnership mechanism now operating in the student aid programs. SSIG is a matching program that offers states federal matching funds in return for state investment in need-based grant funding. SSIG is generally credited with helping to stimulate significant investment in state grant programs at an extremely affordable price to the federal government. For example, in 1989–90 the program provided $72 million in incentive funds to the states. In that same year states awarded approximately $1.6 billion in need-based grant dollars, or more than twenty dollars for every federal matching dollar.

In recent years, however, growing public policy pressure has been exerted to phase out the program. Critics contend with some justification that the SSIG program has served its purpose and is no longer needed. For example, whereas SSIG funding held relatively stable throughout most of the 1980s (at around $70 million), state grant spending more than doubled. Further, most states significantly overmatch the federal contribution. This situation suggests that state grant funding is on a track independent of the incentives offered through SSIG.

Despite the apparently declining importance of SSIG in stimulating new investment in grant programs by the states, there are several important reasons why the mechanism of incentive funding should be retained. First, because it is an extant vehicle, there is no need to argue (in the public policy context) for a new, perhaps costly program. Second, though most states do overmatch SSIG allocations, about ten states remain at or near the required 50 percent minimum state match. These include Alabama, the District of Columbia, Mississippi, and other states where access to higher education has been a difficult uphill battle (and where cuts in federal funding could therefore be disastrous). Third, with the proper incentives, significant new funds earmarked for higher education assistance could be generated at a modest cost to the federal government. In fact, with the proper modifications, SSIG could be significantly revitalized to generate new funding and to provide new goals and opportunities for the partnership. Thus, changes to the SSIG mechanism that work to build on the success of SSIG in the past and give it new vigor and promise for the future need to be enacted.

One way to make such a change would be to alter the incentive structure. For example, states might be required to increase their spending on state grants based on an index of college cost increases. SSIG matching funds would not be allowed unless states ensured that grant funding kept pace with the price paid by students. This would be an especially effective way of better serving the population currently participating in state grant programs.

Ideally, however, federal policy should be geared toward achieving two goals: expanding the pool of persons eligible to receive aid money—thereby improving access for a broader range of students—and ensuring that the amount of funds provided is sufficient to cover reasonable student expenses. To meet these objectives, the federal government might consider taking a more aggressive, but not necessarily much more costly, approach to partnership. If the matching requirement was changed to stimulate even greater nonfederal spending, for instance, the opportunities for access could be improved considerably. Here are two possible approaches to this altered matching process.

First, the match could be changed to require greater spending on the part of the states. Combined with an increase in federal matching funds, significant new funds could be generated. If the federal government doubled its investment in SSIG from the 1989–90 level ($72 million) and required that this funding be matched on a forty-sixty federal-state basis, approximately $108 million in new state grant spending would be created. Although at first glance this sum may seem rather modest, the new match would significantly benefit those states that currently do not overmatch federal SSIG funding. On the one hand, the need-based state grant spending of California, which has a very large program, would increase by only about 17 percent under this new matching formula; on the other, both Alabama and Mississippi would register increases in the 120 percent range. Thus, the new matching requirement would be most effective in those states where significant additional investment in state grant spending is needed.

The other way to change the process would be to bring a new partner into the SSIG system. If institutions, for example, were required to match federal incentive funding at the same rate as states, even greater grant funding levels could be generated. If, as above, current spending levels and matches stayed the same (a $72 million federal allocation matched by a $72 million state allocation) and if an identical amount were matched again by both the states and institutions, the benefits could be significant: in California, state grant spending would continue to increase rather modestly (20 percent), but in Alabama and Mississippi it would jump nearly 150 percent.

One obvious concern about the second approach, however, is that the institution's role is unclear. Would institutions be required to award the matching money directly to students, or would the "match" simply be paid to the state? Similarly, would institutions be penalized for nonparticipation, and if so, how? These and other questions will need to be addressed.

One way to cement the relationship of institutions within the SSIG partnership would be to make them an integral part of a new approach to incentive funding. If institutions played a major part in an SSIG program that had more than just increased state grant spending as its goal, then the institutional contribution/participation might be a linchpin in the entire process.

There have been many proposals for altering the purposes and goals of SSIG, ranging from making it a program that encourages student choice to one that targets adult and nontraditional students. However, the option that has garnered the most public policy interest is the one that ties SSIG to state-level early-intervention or early-awareness programs. If SSIG could be given the goal of encouraging young, at-risk children to stay in school and prepare academically for college, and if it could contain adequate assurances that substantial financial support would be available at the time of entrance to college, SSIG would be endowed with a significant, timely new purpose.

SSIG could be used to create a national early-intervention program, coordinated by the federal government, administered by the states, and financed through contributions from institutions, private sources, and the federal and state governments. Federal contributions could be combined with state and other funding in order to create state-level endowment funds. States would use these funds for several purposes. They could be used for the costs of counseling and outreach services, or the funds could be invested to help pay for scholarships for program participants who make it to college. Program participants could be identified at an early age, perhaps sixth grade, and supported and encouraged throughout their academic careers.

Institutions could serve several functions: they could furnish sites for remedial and tutorial services, offer skilled personnel to act as tutors or mentors, and provide campus visits and tours for program participants. Institutions might also establish relationships with school districts through which, by contributing to the statewide endowment, they would pay for early-intervention services for a set number of students. The colleges would guarantee that students who successfully complete the program would be assured admission and substantial tuition assistance.

Increasing Risk Sharing in Federal Student Loans

The federally guaranteed student loan programs under Part B of the Higher Education Act depend on several partners to deliver loans to students. Private lenders originate loans and thereby furnish the capital needed to award money to students. Secondary markets provide liquidity by buying loan paper from these lenders. Institutions counsel students and are held responsible for keeping default levels down or risk losing their eligibility to receive federal student aid funds. State-level agencies insure the loans against default for lenders, thereby reducing the risk to lenders. And finally, to further minimize risk, the federal government reinsures the guarantees made by guarantee agencies.

This seemingly complex web of partners and responsibilities, however, belies a basic simplicity of the federally guaranteed student loan system. Because of the near-absolute guarantee made by the federal government, the risk to the other partners is comparatively minor. Although there is certainly accountability in the system—for example, the institutional default cutoff—the reality is that only modest standards need to be met in order to reap the significant benefits of the federal guarantee. One respected analyst, economist Barry Bosworth, has gone so far as to label the system a fraud; he contends that the federal guarantee acts to preserve the profits of loan system participants.

If, as many have argued, the student loan system portrays itself as market-based but does not allow for any real market effects, then adjustments should be made to the structure. Assuming that the basic design and content of the student loan system is retained, several modifications could be made. Many of these would convert the existing system from one where disparate sets of mostly self-interested partners vie for position to one in which all partners share the risks (and rewards) of providing student loans.

For example, institutions, which for the first time are being held accountable for extreme levels of default by students attending their institution, could be held to other standards. The default-rate cutoff might be reduced to a level below the 35 percent "cohort rate" calculation now in effect. Likewise, institutions might be compelled to forgo some part of loan revenues until student aid recipients complete a significant portion of the program of study, thereby increasing the institution's stake (to a reasonable degree) in their success.

Another possible change might concern the guarantee agencies. These have been held to a basic standard of accountability for several years. Agencies with an annual rate of default (by the students whose loans they guarantee) above a congressionally prescribed level receive less than 100 percent reinsurance from the federal government. These agencies receive either a 90 or 80 percent rate of reinsurance, depending on the severity of the defaults beyond the federal "trigger."

This system is commendable, but it is not without defects. There is some reason to believe that guarantee agencies have only a limited amount of influence on the defaults on the student loans in their portfolio. In fact, there is some anecdotal evidence to suggest that the greater the age of the guarantee agency and the maturity of the loan paper in its portfolio, the less likely the agency is to reach the federal trigger.

One way to correct this possible inequity and at the same time inject greater risk sharing among agencies would be to eliminate the 100 percent reinsurance provision, perhaps lowering it to 95 percent. This change would place all agencies on a more equal basis because all would have to generate some level of self-support funding. It also serves as a concrete way of proving that the state's role is not part of the fraud, as Bosworth might argue, but is in fact a viable component of the partnership.

Yet the partner that needs to increase its share of the risk is by far the lender of guaranteed loans. A powerful consumer banking lobby in Washington has been effective for many years in keeping the risk-sharing forces at bay. The thrust of the lobby's argument has been that any significant changes to the current system of guarantees and incentives would result in a massive pull out from the loan programs by lenders. Further, the lobby has contended that because of the detailed procedural requirements placed on lenders by the federal government (the so-called due-diligence regulations), their profitability in these programs has been marginal.

To understand the import of these arguments, it is necessary to describe the benefits from the program that accrue to lenders. First, barring a failure to follow due-diligence requirements, lenders are fully guaranteed against student defaults (that is, the process of lending is virtually risk-free). Second, lenders are paid a "special allowance" by the federal government in order to ensure a market rate of return on loans. This allowance amounts to a direct payment for program participation—hardly a market-based system, as has been noted. Third, lenders are encouraged through Sallie Mae (a government-sponsored enterprise) or other secondary-market agencies to sell their loans to these agencies at a discount. This system allows the agencies to have an adequate level of liquidity to make new loans—an important advantage—but it also permits lenders to pay little personal attention to the borrowers. The ability to sell loans quickly also reduces the lenders' risk.

One of the inherent contradictions of the lender role in the guaranteed loan programs recently came to light when the Bush administration floated a proposal to create a national student loan bank, with the federal government providing the capital to make loans. The administration claimed that eliminating the banks from the process would greatly reduce federal-subsidy costs, particularly as they relate to the special allowance. The banks were then forced to argue—in the context of the high rate of bank failures across the country (which began as the savings-and-loan crisis)—that an elimination of the bank-based loan system would have seriously deleterious effects on the banking system. In other words, banks had to concede that the loan programs do provide them with a reasonable level of profit, a contradiction of their long-standing claim.

Banks should, of course, also be held to standards of accountability and share in the risks as well as the benefits of the loan system. One way to produce this outcome would be to reduce the 100 percent rate of insurance, perhaps by holding banks—like institutions—to some minimum standard of default. This change would increase the stake that banks have in establishing a long-term relationship with students, thereby helping to avoid defaults.

Another way to increase the lenders' risks in the programs—and achieve budgetary savings—would be to cut the rate of special allowance. But rather than simply setting the special allowance at a fixed reduced level (as has been sought by other analysts), a sliding scale might be implemented instead. For example, lenders could be paid a rate commensurate with past performance. Performance would be measured by such indicators as default levels, diversity of students served, and percentage of total loan paper sold to secondary markets.

Strengthening the System of Institutional Eligibility

Yet another way to strengthen and refine the student aid partnership would be to change the way colleges and schools are approved for the receipt of federal student aid monies. This system currently has three components, which are sometimes called the oversight "triad." The three components are accreditation, state licensing, and federal eligibility/certification. Schools desiring to participate in federal student aid programs must meet the standards of each.

Because it is generally associated with the setting of standards that relate to the educational mission of an institution, accreditation has generally been considered the "gatekeeper" of institutional eligibility for student aid. As such, the federal government has contended that accrediting agencies are the closest to the services provided by an institution and therefore are best qualified to assess it. This is not to say that the federal government has no interest in, or connection to, the quality of an educational program being paid for with student aid funds. The federal government indirectly influences quality by sanctioning certain accrediting agencies. These agencies must be included on an approved list in order for the federal government to accept their finding about a school.

State licensing is currently the weakest component of the triad. The federal government merely requires that schools be licensed by the state in which they operate. It does not hold states to any set of minimum standards. Not surprisingly, these vary considerably across states and are generally not difficult to meet.

Finally, the federal government does have its own two-step process for approving institutions for student aid. The first step is referred to as *eligibility,* whereby the U.S. Department of Education checks to make certain that the school is accredited and licensed. The submission of various written materials, such as a statement of the academic credit system, a copy of the institution's tuition refund policy, and a recent school catalogue, is also required. Schools meeting the eligibility standard then must meet a *certification* standard. Here, the Education Department examines the administrative and financial capabilities of an institution. Like the eligibility process, certification is almost exclusively a paper-based system.

One fundamental problem with the triad approach is that it places the largest degree of control in the hands of the only nongovernmental members, the accrediting bodies. Further, there is no coordination (and in many cases no contact) among the various members. Also, the failure to define any standards for the states means that the federal government has no influence on state licensing policy or practice. These shortcomings in the triad process help to explain why (according to a report by the U.S. Senate Permanent Investigations Subcommittee) 97 percent of all schools that apply for federal student aid eligibility are approved.

Institutions that are able to become eligible to receive federal student aid monies have a significant and (in the case of the federal loan programs) nearly bottomless pool from which to draw tuition revenues. Without constraints on the amount they may charge students (beyond annual aid maximums) and in the absence of any controls over the ways in which they educate students for the prices they charge, institutions have become increasingly dependent on federal aid. This has been especially true for proprietary institutions, 80 percent of whose students receive federal aid (the sum of which accounts for about a third of all federal aid awarded to students).

The solutions to these dilemmas lie largely with the members of the triad themselves. For example, accrediting agencies need to accept more explicitly their quasi-governmental role and take more responsibility for their actions as they relate to the reliance of schools on student aid funds. More frequent reviews of institutions, more detailed examinations of schools that have been "flagged" because of potential problems, and more willingness to deny accreditation and reaccreditation outright should be instituted.

The place where the most reform can and should occur, though, is at the state level. National standards for licensing, based not on specific "model" legislation or regulations but on a series of universal principles, should be established. These national standards should be developed by statewide coordinating and governing boards for higher education, with significant input from institutions, employers, and others.

The federal government also needs to expand its own role and to improve the coordination of the partnership. Not only should the standards governing the administrative and financial capabilities of institutions be raised (including more detailed, on-site reviews), but the requirements placed on the other partners should also be tightened. For instance, the federal government could stipulate that accrediting organizations furnish verified outcomes information (information on the retention, graduation, and/or job placement of students, verified by an independent authority) as well as justifications for creating a new institution or program and the qualifications of faculty and other staff. Similarly, states can be required to establish minimum standards for state licensing (perhaps in the form of a statement of principles, as above) or to designate a single state agency as the one primarily responsible for ensuring that schools are properly licensed. These and other broad federal requirements would greatly strengthen the triad's overall effectiveness while maintaining the integrity of each of its component members.

Conclusion

Partnership is a concept that has been frequently discussed in the context of improving the national network of student aid programs. And yet, in the nearly two decades since the greatest commitment to equal educational opportunity was made—the passage of the Pell Grant program in 1972—few concrete steps have been taken to improve this partnership. In fact, in those few instances where greater cooperation and coordination among the various players has occurred—as with the requirement placed on institutions to keep loan default levels down—the cooperation has developed largely because of immediately pressing budgetary, rather than educational, concerns. Improvement in the delivery and targeting of student aid has thus been accorded a lower public-policy priority than the one for educational quality.

Though cynics may contend that budgetary considerations affect nearly all public policy, the reality is that student aid policies driven by fiscal imperatives have resulted in declining public confidence and support for those programs and a lack of clear indicators about their success. To continue down this perilous road will likely lead to even further declines. This is a particularly troubling thought given the growing challenges, both demographic and political, that face American higher education in the coming decade.

A strengthened partnership would benefit all participants, but in particular the students for whom aid programs were designed. These students' success or failure will ultimately decide whether a national strategy of equalizing educational opportunity, developed and implemented by the federal government, states, institutions, and others, has been worth the considerable investment of time and resources.

Jamie P. Merisotis is a higher education consultant in Washington, D.C.

Complexity of the current application and aid delivery system is helping to motivate efforts to simplify the process that culminates in the awarding of student aid.

Simplification of Need Analysis and Aid Delivery: Imperatives and Opportunities

Brian K. Fitzgerald

Simplification of the processes by which student aid is awarded has been a long-sought, yet elusive goal. No single component of the student aid process has received as much attention, nor generated as much controversy, as the need-analysis formulas that determine financial eligibility for federal and other student aid programs. This debate continues today and, as the reauthorization of the Higher Education Act (HEA) approaches, the student aid community appears poised to support simplification of both formulas for determining need and the broader processes for delivering this financial aid to students.

Despite the emergence of widespread support for simplification, agreement on the details of how to simplify may fail to coalesce if the history of this issue is any indication. Simplification of need analysis has not been achieved, in large measure, because it touches many deeply rooted values and uniquely American political arrangements. The structure of the federal programs reflects American commitment to equality and equity. Since the inception of the programs in 1965, the nation has invested hundreds of billions of dollars to promote equality of educational opportunity. Further, the structure of need analysis, particularly its progressivity, reflects a commitment to equity that is shared with, for example, the federal tax system. At the same time, the general structure of need-based federal student aid reflects the fact that the primary responsibility for financing postsecondary

The views expressed in this chapter are those of the author, and no official support by the Advisory Committee on Student Financial Assistance or other government entity is intended or should be inferred.

education lies with the individual, in sharp contrast with elementary and secondary education.

The manner in which Congress confronts the numerous sensitive issues involved in simplification holds significant implications not only for the federal government, but also for institutions of postsecondary education, student aid professionals, and students and families. This chapter reviews the attempts to simplify student aid and the barriers that have frustrated such efforts. It also assesses four opportunities that have arisen as a result of recent policy changes: simplification of need-analysis formulas; integration of the formulas; streamlining of reapplication; and alteration of the basis for regulating the programs.

Federal Role in Need Analysis and Delivery

The passage of the Higher Education Act of 1965 established the federal government's specialized role of providing low-income students access to postsecondary education through financial aid. The student aid delivery system, however, posed particular problems for the federal government. As with many of the Great Society programs, the urgency of the perceived national needs outweighed practical concerns. In considering student aid Congress eschewed key questions of design and delivery; consequently, in the hectic period after the passage of the HEA, federal administrators looked to existing systems of need analysis provided by the College Board and the American College Testing Program and to colleges and universities to award and deliver aid under the new federal programs.

These systems had their roots in ground-breaking work conducted during the 1940s and 1950s. Through consensus among selective private colleges, these systems prevented overawarding of scholarship aid in the period before the creation of the federal student aid programs. Early empirical studies, for example, examined the manner in which families of Harvard undergraduates financed their education. This work provided the underpinnings of the formulas used to determine need for many programs, including federal and many state and institutional student aid programs today.

Congress and the higher education community again faced complex issues related to the structure of the formulas during the creation of the Basic Educational Opportunity Grant (now the Pell Grant) program. For the first time, however, federal policy discussions explicitly considered the feasibility of utilizing a four- or five-element formula to deliver aid to the neediest students. The weight of opinion held that such simple formulas were not sufficiently sensitive to deliver aid and would inadvertently fund wealthier students who might appear needy based on only a few data elements. Thus, a more complex formula with much more data was required.

As Congress developed the Pell Grant program, it made an explicit choice to fund students directly according to a predetermined award schedule rather than allocating funds to institutions, as in the Campus-Based programs. Although it fashioned the Pell Grant eligibility formula from existing need-analysis methods, Congress retained control. The higher education community, fearing the manipulation of the formula as a budget tool, decried the creation of a new system.

In the mid-1970s, the community took an important step toward achieving simplification by empaneling the Keppel Task Force (formally called the National Task Force on Student Aid Problems), whose goal was to determine a single need-analysis formula to replace the dozens that existed for awarding Campus-Based funds. The task force also sought to devise a single application form. Both goals were important because students who applied to multiple institutions faced many different forms and formulas, which produced varying family contributions and therefore a range of aid packages. (These differences were large enough in the years preceding the Keppel Task Force to prompt hearings on the formulas by Congress.) Although the task force created a single need-analysis formula for the Campus-Based programs—not without considerable difficulty—many vestiges of previous problems still existed. The Pell Grant program continued to use a separate formula. In addition, some institutions, most notably selective private institutions, continued to use subtly different formulas that required additional data.

In the decade following the completion of the Keppel Task Force's work, researchers attempted to identify means of simplifying need-analysis methods. Efforts ranged from utilizing statistical techniques to identify a set of fewer data elements that would most closely approximate the results of the full formula, to developing a framework for evaluating individual data elements in the formula. The latter effort assessed the contributions of key dimensions, including effects on the federal budget, redistribution of program funds by type of recipients, sensitivity, verifiability, and reliability of data. Researchers and policy analysts conducted many analyses of alternative systems. However, despite analytical advances, this research produced little progress toward simplification.

At the same time, national studies conducted throughout the 1980s by the Department of Education examined the accuracy of the data supplied by applicants and used by institutions. Inaccurate data—whether due to confusion because of the complexity of the formula or application instructions, or to conscious manipulation—affected the awards that individual applicants received and, potentially, the level of all awards. Consequently, the Keppel Task Force urged verification efforts as early as the mid-1970s. But the Department of Education's studies, although criticized and ultimately dismissed by many in the higher education community as politically motivated, also posed a dramatic new criterion that must be taken into account as data elements and formulas are evaluated. The degree to which the apparent equity and sensitivity of a formula are achieved is a function of the accuracy of the data (though the actual equity and sensitivity effects may be substantially different in reality).

Characteristics of the Policy Debate

Several principles characterized the policy debate from the initiation of the federal government's role in need-based student aid through the mid-1980s. Each had its roots in theory or practice that either predated or emerged during this period. The search for a unitary system was the most fundamental characteristic of the period. In such a system, students applying for financial aid would be judged on the same basis, using the same data and preferably the same formula. If student aid professionals were forced to deal with a separate system for the Pell Grant program, they could at least avoid multiple formulas for the other programs. The work of the Keppel Task Force perhaps best exemplified the community's commitment to the unitary system of need analysis. The devising of a single need-analysis model, the so-called Uniform Methodology, from the dozens of competing models that existed at the time represents the task force's greatest achievement. The consensus among the diverse membership of the task force also permitted the creation of an application form on which students and parents would submit data for use in calculating state and institutional awards.

The Uniform Methodology also embodied the principle of equality: that all students at all types of institutions should be judged not only by standard rules, but also by precisely the same formula and even the same application process. Students, families, and institutions would benefit from the elimination of the mélange of applications and systems. The approach had other implications, however. No applicant, not even the poorest of those attending institutions in the emerging public sector, could be excused from being judged by a complex formula, whose roots were in middle- and upper-class patterns of financing private education.

The creation of the Uniform Methodology demonstrated the primacy of one principle on which the formula was based: sensitivity. To determine effectively the ability of an individual family to pay for education, any need-based formula would require the capacity to make fine distinctions among applicants. The most significant test of a formula thus became pair-wise comparisons; these involved comparing families that appeared similar on one set of data items (such as income, family size, and number in college) but different on another set (including assets, the number of parents working, and unusual expenses).

Throughout the period of the 1970s and early 1980s, pair-wise equity emerged as the crucial litmus test and fundamental decision-making paradigm. Formulas or changes to them would have to withstand rigorous pair-wise tests, in which the treatment of subtly different theoretical applicants appeared equitable to the practitioner and policymaker alike. The emphasis on the pair-wise-equity paradigm increased pressure during the period to find fairer treatment for families with relatively unique circumstances, such as unusual medical or elementary and secondary tuition expenses as a means of ensuring the sensitivity and thereby the equity of the formula.

Such evaluations of alternative systems or treatments, particularly those aimed at simplifying need analysis, were constrained by two factors, however. First, these evaluations used the observed outcomes of the Uniform Methodology. The Keppel Task Force participants had made explicit their concern about the accuracy of the data submitted by applicants and endorsed verification of these data. Yet despite this concern and increasing voluntary use of verification by practitioners, analyses were conducted on observed outcomes produced by originally submitted, unverified data. Second, unlike analyses and simulations conducted in the Pell Grant program, which measured the impact on awards of changes to the formula, efforts to simplify the Uniform Methodology examined changes in family contributions. Such contributions are but one factor in determining Campus-Based awards, which may vary much more substantially for a given contribution level than Pell Grants. Thus, the impact of simplification on awards was not well understood.

Ultimately, the emphasis on the pair-wise-equity paradigm for evaluating simplification alternatives fostered a belief that fairness in the programs must be achieved through need analysis per se. The assessments of various formulas and therefore, more broadly, the decision-making framework, were unable to link an array of family contributions to awards and precluded the consideration of other components of the delivery of Campus-Based and other aid, including institutional-packaging policies and procedures.

Through the early 1980s the debate surrounding need analysis and, more specifically, simplification, sought to achieve macroequality through a unitary system of need analysis. At the same time, evaluators approached this need-analysis system within a pair-wise-equity paradigm that was to ensure microequity. As the 1980s progressed, two forces—increasing pressure to simplify need analysis and tensions between the executive branch and the Congress over reducing expenditures and eliminating programs—presaged a series of events that would reshape key aspects of the student aid policy debate.

Current Policy Context

If central features of the need-analysis-formula debate were best addressed in the work of the Keppel Task Force, no single event demonstrates the fundamental alteration of that policy debate more clearly than the passage of the Higher Education Amendments of 1986. The reauthorization of student aid programs in that year altered the governance of the programs, the structure of need analysis and aid delivery, and, ultimately, the basis for evaluating the effectiveness of need analysis and delivery.

In reauthorizing the Title IV programs in 1986, Congress reacted to half a decade of dispute between the executive and legislative branches by altering the relationship among the parties in the student aid governance structure. In this regard, writing need analysis into statute represented perhaps Congress's most significant action because it removed the student aid community's authority over one of the basic components of the delivery system. Altering features of need analysis through community consensus—using mechanisms such as the Keppel Task Force—would no longer be possible. In an action that may have produced the greatest deterioration in the governing structure, Congress prohibited the Secretary of Education from issuing regulations related to either the Pell Grant or Congressional Methodology (CM) formulas. Taken together, these steps brought federal need analysis firmly under congressional control.

At the same time Congress also took significant steps toward making the Pell Grant and CM systems more similar, particularly by aligning their application data requirements. The predecessor to the CM—the Uniform Methodology—used data, specifically income items, that were different from the Pell Grant formula.

In addition, Congress took a major step toward simplifying need analysis, if only for a portion of the applicant population. Based on research conducted by the Department of Education in the mid-1980s, Congress created an approach for primarily low-income applicants that eliminated assets from the formula (which few of these students report). The Department of Education's research had demonstrated that few applicants who qualify for the simple need analysis would receive different awards using that method than with the full Pell Grant formula or Congressional Methodology; indeed, virtually none received a different Pell Grant.

The invention of simplified need analysis signaled a repudiation of key features of the policy consensus that had existed prior to 1986. First, although Congress embraced aspects of the unitary system, particularly by making the structure of the Pell Grant and Congressional Methodology more similar, it clearly departed from a unitary system as it related to the treatment of individual students. Before 1986 all aid applicants were subjected to the same need analysis formulas; however, after the implementation of the Congressional Methodology, need analysis was more tailored to the circumstances of groups of applicants. Congress further repudiated the unitary system by tailoring the formula for two groups with unique needs: women returning to the work force and workers unemployed because of plant closings.

At the same time that Congress reshaped the principles underlying need analysis, both from a governance and a structural perspective, it signaled new federal priorities for the delivery process. The Higher Education Amendments required the Department of Education to contract with processors to process student aid applications at no cost to students and to ensure that the application form was common across all processors. Although these contracts had existed since the late 1970s and the statute contained the requirement for a common, no-fee form, Congress now required a form and application process that was standard regardless of which processor the student used to apply for aid. Before 1986 forms had been tailored by processors to meet the unique needs of constituent institutions and states, as well as to conform to the Uniform Methodology.

New Imperatives

In taking these steps, Congress fundamentally altered the framework within which need analysis, and indeed the delivery system, was evaluated. If the status quo ante had stressed microequity in need analysis and the organization of the delivery system flowed from this, the new order ushered in by the 1986 amendments sought a balance between broad program goals and microequity. The difference in emphasis is perhaps nowhere more evident than in the refocusing of need analysis evaluation toward broad program goals. Previously, microequity had been assured by maximizing the sensitivity of the formula to individual differences, particularly through pair-wise comparisons. In sharp contrast, congressional actions taken in the 1986 amendments reflected the perspective that the effectiveness of need analysis should be evaluated on the basis of ability to achieve broad program goals. Within this new context a need-analysis system that created barriers for key applicant subpopulations could not be judged to be effective even if it produced high levels of sensitivity for most recipients. Congress demonstrated a willingness to make an unprecedented trade-off: a minor diminution in the sensitivity of the formula in exchange for promotion of broader program goals.

The unwillingness of Congress to accept burdens on low-income populations may have represented the most fundamental and emotional aspect of the changes. A single need-analysis system for the Campus-Based programs that subjected welfare families and upper-income, professional families to the same burden and cost was no longer deemed acceptable. Some in the financial aid community claimed, however, that the burden on low-income applicants associated with "zero-filling" numerous items and that the cost of submitting applications did not pose serious barriers to these applicants. In addition, many claimed that a separate, simpler formula for low-income applicants created complexity for all applicants. Finally, serious questions persisted concerning the value of need analysis to the lowest income students, as most were eligible for maximum aid.

Congress's new approach to need analysis also had implications for the broad delivery process. The data needs of institutions and states represented a key rationale for utilizing the integrated delivery procedures pioneered by the Keppel Task Force. However, federal aid had now emerged as the single largest share of available aid, and Congress was no longer willing to subordinate emergent federal programmatic and delivery priorities to those of institutions and states.

Congress also responded to two emerging factors: changing demographics and the increasing public perception of complexity. The actual and projected decline in the numbers of traditional higher education students—white middle-class—and the growth of low-income and minority students pose serious challenges to the student aid programs. Indeed, minority students, many of whom will be low-income, will form the majority in postsecondary education in several states shortly after the turn of the century. This projected growth comes in the face of widespread complaints about the complexity of the application process: respondents to a recent survey found only the IRS tax forms and state tax forms more complex than aid applications. In addition, families increasingly recognize the importance of student aid and feel they could not afford postsecondary education without such assistance. Perceptions of the complexity and importance of student aid have combined to produce an uncertainty that undermines public confidence in the programs.

Finally, the increasingly broad and pervasive implications of regulations present another serious motivation to simplify the programs. Since the early 1980s numerous regulations have burdened parents and students, as well as practitioners. This burden has taxed program delivery, frustrated students and parents, and cost institutions millions of dollars.

There are two major reasons why regulations have mushroomed over the past decade: verification of student aid application data and procedures to combat student loan defaults. Together, they characterize the crush of regulations that is being felt by many students at virtually all institutions and illustrate the complexity of the debate that pits regulatory relief against accountability.

As part of efforts to improve the efficiency of government during the Carter and Reagan administrations, various agencies began a series of quality-control initiatives. These activities were aimed at increasing the accuracy of program delivery by eliminating ineligible recipients from program rolls and ensuring that recipients received the proper benefits. In the Title IV programs these activities began in 1978 with a series of pilot studies, which determined that the data used in the Pell Grant program were often inaccurate—resulting in the erroneous awarding (usually, but not always, to eligible, needy students) of hundreds of millions of dollars.

In response the Department of Education immediately initiated a series of policies that required institutions to verify the data that students submitted on their applications for the Pell Grant program. Although at the outset Department of Education regulations required verification of only a few data items for relatively few students, verification levels increased rapidly. In academic year 1980–81, verification was limited to 325,000 applicants (or 7.2 percent of all applicants). In 1982–83, responding to quality-control study findings, the number increased to 1.66 million Pell Grant applicants, a figure representing more than 60 percent of all applicants; and the department planned to expand the substantiation of selected data to all Pell Grant applicants. In years following, the Department of Education imposed verification procedures on all programs, and in the 1986–87 academic year the Department of Education began to investigate an expanded number of data items for all applicants. Throughout this period the financial aid community brought significant pressure to bear on Congress to reduce verification levels, which caused the Department of Education to scale back its plans. Finally, the Education Amendments of 1986 limited verification to a maximum of 30 percent of all applicants, and the department's plan to substantiate the information provided by all applicants was jettisoned. Nevertheless, verification activities today constitute a major commitment of resources on campuses and a major problem and source of frustration for parents and students.

Relatively recently, default reduction has become a major source of concern. Since the mid-1980s, with Stafford Loan and Supplemental Loans for Students (SLS) default costs growing from $1 billion to more than $3 billion, defaults have dominated policy discussions and proposals. The Department of Education has sought to impose various regulations designed to reduce defaults, the most controversial of which was the 20 percent institutional default cap. The cap threatened to eliminate hundreds of institutions—proprietary, two-year, and historically minority—from Title IV participation. Due to the controversy and a new secretary of education, the single cap was replaced by a graduated cap, which mandated increasingly stringent requirements for higher default-rate institutions and termination of participation at 60 percent. The plan met with general approval in the higher education community as well as in the Congress.

Ironically, these regulations have not halted the efforts to control default through additional program changes and regulation. This outcome is largely the result of the very characteristics that made the default-reduction regulations acceptable, indeed popular: the objectives of regulations often take years to achieve when reasonable approaches are used, particularly when the regulations utilize self-improvement techniques.

The Department of Education also has tried through regulation to control program abuse that contributes to default. Propelled by several inspector general reports, which identify abuses in the proprietary sector, the department recently released proposed regulations that would control the practice of lengthening programs to qualify for more federal aid by establishing a minimum of hours for each program credit. The department reasoned that the limitation would in part reduce the indebtedness of vocational students (whose courses at many proprietary institutions are measured in contact or clock hours) and thereby reduce default. The regulation would apply to all programs that award less than an associate or baccalaureate degree. However, the regulation would have profound implications for community colleges, which measure most vocational courses in credit hours and were not the target of the regulations. These courses would be required to have the number of contact hours specified in the regulation, rather than the number historically required. At a minimum, community colleges would have to undertake a complete review of courses to determine the exact number of contact hours in each program.

The institutions at which the regulation was targeted (proprietary institutions) would be free to reconfigure courses to meet the new requirements and therefore would be largely unhurt by the regulation. In an unprecedented, if potentially unconstitutional action, Congress ordered the comment period on the proposed rule extended past the statutory publication date by which regulations must be finalized to be effective for the following academic year; the effect was to kill the regulation for the present.

However, default reduction represents a fundamentally different policy process in comparison to verification. Although virtually the entire verification initiative resulted from the Department of Education's actions, Congress has fully joined—and in many ways led—the default-reduction effort. In early 1986 Congress sponsored a default-reduction conference at Belmont, Maryland. Concerned by embarrassingly large default costs, consistent program abuse scandals, and the failure of the nation's largest agency for guaranteeing federal student loans, Congress has enacted a series of program alterations, mostly through the budget process, designed to reduce defaults and default costs. These program changes have limited eligibility for the SLS program, required entrance and exit interviews with borrowers, mandated the maintenance and publication of program completion data, restricted admission of non–high school graduates to eligible institutions through alteration of the ability-to-benefit provision, and, most recently, required delayed disbursement of Stafford loans to all first-time borrowers.

These changes (many of which must be implemented through regulation) demonstrate that default legislation also has the potential for imposing substantial burden. Indeed, the recent budget reconciliation provisions raise serious practical, financial, governance, and constitutional questions. Collection and publication of program-completion rates pose serious practical problems for community colleges, which may be required to track every student that is enrolled in a single noncredit course. Delayed disbursement for all first-time borrowers has created major financial and legal problems. Many private, tuition-driven institutions, some already under tremendous pressure to control costs, will face a loss of revenue as a result of the delay. In addition, many public institutions are prohibited by state law from permitting students to enroll who have not remitted all necessary funds.

The complexity that confronts all who use or observe the need-analysis and the delivery systems results from many sources. Complicated, competing need-analysis models that require large amounts of data annually—data that must be verified—produce inefficiency. The impending change in demographics present even greater challenges. As we have seen, efforts to address serious programmatic issues such as default through regulation and legislation, the effects of which often are indiscriminate, have proven onerous, particularly to some institutions that have not contributed to the problem.

Opportunities to Simplify

Taken together, the complex characteristics of the current system present a strong incentive to simplify need analysis and the delivery process. At the same time, the breadth of these characteristics suggests that efforts to address complexity through simplification must be equally broad. Uncharacteristically, a wide series of options now exist and are under serious discussion as reauthorization approaches. Many stand to improve delivery; all require trade-offs of some kind. The willingness of the various parties in the political process to accept these compromises will determine whether these opportunities are seized upon. Similarly, the willingness of the parties involved in program delivery to accept trade-offs ultimately will determine whether simplification is actually achieved or merely legislated.

For virtually every source of complexity, there is a corresponding policy alternative that would reduce the burden on many of the parties in the delivery process. These policy options include (1) further simplifying the existing need-analysis models, (2) integrating the competing need-analysis models, (3) streamlining delivery procedures, particularly the reapplication process, and (4) altering the approach to regulating. Although they are not the only possibilities, these options have the potential for reducing complexity most substantially.

Simplifying Need Analysis

Achieving simplification through adjustments to existing need-analysis models represents one of the best, though potentially controversial, opportunities. For nearly two decades the financial aid community, the Department of Education, and Congress have debated simplification of need-analysis formulas. While this debate shows great interest, it also indicates that the numerous parties in the policy process have disparate views that may be difficult to reconcile.

Nevertheless, in the period preceding congressional reauthorization activities, many groups have begun to develop and analyze simplification alternatives. These alternatives appear to be aligned along a continuum, ranging from modest expansions of the current simplified need analysis to wholesale replacement of the current formulas. Several of the alternatives discussed below demonstrate the range of the approaches to the problem.

Expansion of the number of individuals eligible for simplified need analysis, including families of dependent students, represents one solution. Under the current program rules, families and individuals with adjusted gross incomes of under $15,000 may use the simplified need analysis. This shortened formula excludes from the calculation all assets as well as certain allowable expenses, which effectively lower income. Increasing the income cap for qualification would expand the number of individuals eligible to use simplified need analysis.

The most conservative of the many alternatives would permit modest growth in the number of eligible individuals by increasing the income cap to adjust for the inflation that has occurred since the act was last reauthorized. However, merely adjusting for inflation would only ensure that the original target population remains eligible. Other proposals would increase the income cap further, perhaps to as high as $30,000.

One such proposal is the result of several years work by the Need Analysis Standards Committee of the National Association of Student Financial Aid Administrators (NASFAA). Beginning in 1987, this committee began exploring existing research in an effort to construct a single, simplified need-analysis formula that could be used by all families and for all federal programs. The committee's approach included developing a new nomenclature—as the existing nomenclature was highly "value-laden"—and scrapping virtually all aspects of the current formulas. In addition, the committee planned to write a separate formula for nonfederal aid programs. In all, the direction chosen by the committee represented an ambitious and commendable effort.

Not surprisingly, however, through the investigatory and consultative process, the alternative formula gravitated toward the existing simplified need analysis. The final proposal, which is different from the structure of the current simplified need analysis in minor but not insignificant ways, will effectively raise the income cap to $25,000.

Several alternatives would expand the approach to simplification outlined above. For the most part, these proposals would identify specific subpopulations of applicants for whom the outcome of need analysis is predictable in advance. These proposals, for example, would exempt from need analysis (but not from filing a form with at least some demographic data) applicants who qualify for means-tested federal human resource programs. Proposals have identified applicants already participating in the Aid to Families with Dependent Children (AFDC) program, in federally subsidized housing programs such as Section Eight housing, in school lunch programs, and several others. Moreover, at least two proposals have identified groups for exemption from need analysis by level of income: one would exempt applicants who had income levels at which they were not required by the IRS to file income taxes; a second would exempt families of dependent students with income below $20,000.

Finally, proposals to replace totally the current long formulas with simplified ones for all applicants have been offered in the past and likely will be again. These proposals most often have substituted a shortened version of the existing long formulas with appropriate adjustments made to avoid major cost increases.

Virtually all of the simplification alternatives, including the current simplified need analysis, have potential implications (real or perceived) for the distribution of aid funds that must be carefully evaluated. Efficiency, sensitivity, accuracy, and redistributional effects are predictably among the criteria that will be used to evaluate these proposals.

Practitioners and policymakers appear to have the least concern about some of the exemption schemes. Clearly, exempting AFDC recipients has widespread support. Proposals to exempt recipients of other means-tested federal human resource programs also have a modicum of support. These alternatives are attractive because they increase the efficiency of the application process for students whose eligibility for student aid is not in doubt. Proposals to exempt applicants from need analysis on the basis of income level enjoy less support. Fears that individuals with high gross income and assets will manipulate the federal tax system to lower net taxable income persist. But the most conservative of these plans would limit exemption to non-tax filers, a solution that would obviate this concern.

Concern with sensitivity, the ability to make fine differentiations among applicants, has been a hallmark of all previous policy discussions concerning simplification. Similar concerns undoubtedly will be raised about the proposals likely to be offered during reauthorization discussions. Logically, the elimination of several data items will reduce the sensitivity of the formulas. However, in this next reauthorization, the effects on individuals will be weighed against broad programwide effects. For example, despite the fact that certain individuals may benefit or be hurt by various alternatives, what will be important is how often these situations arise. Thus, even if some individual awards under the alternative formulas are substantially different than under the existing formulas, the fact that variations occur relatively infrequently would make them inconsequential for policymakers.

Nevertheless, even the relatively small changes in award amounts that result from the current simplified need analysis have raised concerns in the financial aid community. Although there have been minor variations with the Pell Grant formula, they have occurred particularly often with the

Congressional Methodology (CM) because of that formula's unique treatment of assets. Indeed, the fact that a small percentage of applicants eligible to complete the simplified need analysis contributed more under this formula—despite the elimination of all assets—than under the full formula represents a serious problem.

This counterintuitive outcome results from the manner in which assets are treated in the full formula. Some of the first full-scale research on simplification of the Uniform Methodology, from which the CM is a direct descendant, indicated that the assets effectively lower contributions in two-thirds of the cases rather than increasing them as might be assumed (Advanced Technology, 1987). Lowered contributions occur because assets are protected by allowances that increase with the age of the older parent and provide for asset accumulation for retirement. If the level of assets is below the allowable level, the difference reduces income, thus making retirement the first contribution for that family. As many families report assets below the allowable level, the overall effect is to lower contributions.

The redistributional effects of simplification proposals pose a major obstacle to simplification. Not only can the alternative proposals cause redistribution of funds, as demonstrated above, but they also increase the cost of the program. Although these concerns were once the sole province of the executive branch, they are now shared by Congress and the financial aid community—a product of the Gramm-Rudman budget-deficit era. For example, recent analyses of the effect of the NASFAA proposal on Pell Grants indicate that for over 78 percent of recipients the award would be the same, for over 82 percent the difference was within one hundred dollars, and for nearly 89 percent the difference was within two hundred dollars. The majority of the difference increased awards to the recipients—by two to one (Price Waterhouse, 1990). Such outcomes will be scrutinized carefully as the alternatives are evaluated.

The ramifications of a proposal on system accuracy are critical. And some theorists have suggested that several of the alternatives may permit applicants to hide assets. Yet the real effects of a proposal may not be easily determined, particularly when the current formulas are used as comparison points. There is some truth to the fact that the structure of the simplified formulas—eliminating assets, particularly below a specified income level—may make hiding assets possible, but the same and even broader difficulties exist with the current formulas.

Nearly a decade of studies focusing on the accuracy of data supplied by applicants and the implications for awards have demonstrated that the systems as currently structured are highly error-prone. The massive amount of data collected and analyzed, in fact, only provide a false appearance of accuracy and precision. Indeed, analyses conducted by the author (Fitzgerald, 1990) indicate that the system may be so error-prone that a shorter formula with highly verified data may deliver funds to the intended recipients more effectively than the current, full formula. These analyses indicate that when highly verified data are used to determine a distribution of awards for a national sample of over 3,000 Pell Grant recipients, a simplified formula using verified data produces fewer differences—particularly fewer large differences—than the full formula and only moderately verified data. The study demonstrates that not only does reporting error shift the distribution of funds, but this redistribution undermines the purposes of the program: errors shift funds away from lower-income recipients and deliver higher percentages of funds to higher income recipients. These conclusions indicate that evaluating whether a need-analysis formula delivers funds accurately involves broader questions than merely whether certain data elements are included in a formula. Rather, a more thorough examination of the nature, source, and verifiability of data used in the formula is required.

Integrating Need Analysis

The existence of two separate need-analysis formulas and special treatments for such groups as displaced homemakers and dislocated workers contributes substantially to system complexity. Despite Congress's having made the data requirements for the formulas more similar, the ultimate effect has been greater intricacy, both in the numerical outcomes and in distinct program rules necessary for the respective formulas.

Unlike simplification, integration of need analysis has received little analytic attention. This lack of attention has perhaps resulted from the fact that strong structural barriers to integration existed before 1986, when Congress created the Congressional Methodology in statute. Fear of the use of need analysis as a budgetary tool also precluded serious consideration. As reauthorization approaches, however, interest in this area is more widespread.

Several factors are responsible for this increased interest. First, both formulas, Pell and CM, are now under congressional control. Prior to 1986, integration of the general Pell and the (then-used) Uniform Methodology faced not only key analytic problems but also fundamental political difficulties: either the community would be forced to yield control of the UM to the Department of Education or Congress would have to give up control of the Pell Grant program. The previous reauthorization settled the political issue by writing the Uniform Methodology (with important changes) into law. These changes constitute the second factor that has broadened interest in integration. In the process of creating the CM, Congress eliminated many differences in the data used in the two systems. The UM, for example, had used prospective income for all student income. The CM, like Pell Grants, uses prior-tax-year income. These changes eliminated several important differences that contributed to major distortions when one formula was substituted for the other. Finally, the proliferation of formulas—as previously noted, through the creation of special formulas for displaced workers and dislocated homemakers in both Pell and CM—has provided additional motivation for shrinking the number of different calculations that face applicants and practitioners.

A recent examination of integration in the *Journal of Student Financial Aid* represents the most comprehensive assessment of the implications of substituting one of the current formulas for the other. In the lead article, the late Frederick J. Fischer (1990) thoroughly assessed the implications of delivering Pell Grant program awards with the CM. Fischer selects CM as the formula of choice because it is more rooted in theory and generally accepted to be a truer measure of need: Fischer implicitly agrees with a long-held contention that the Pell Grant formula is a rationing device. Ironically, however, Fischer's findings indicate that the CM produces *higher* contributions than the Pell Grant formula. These higher contributions would result in the loss of from several hundred million to perhaps a billion dollars in the Pell Grant program. If there is any fault to be found in this excellent and carefully researched piece, it is that Fischer neglected an obvious and simple alternative: exploring the use of the Pell Grant formula as the most reasonable means of identifying a single existing formula.

This alternative is not without its problems, but it would avoid the most serious implications of his proposal: the regressivity of the effects on recipients. Substitution of the CM with its minimum contribution constitutes a hidden, but no less real, reduction in the minimum award. Fischer demonstrates the tremendous shift that would occur among the most needy population if CM were used to award Pell Grants. Whereas 33 percent of all Pell Grant applicants (about 60 percent of all recipients) have zero contributions, fewer than 5 percent do under the CM. This difference has profound effects on those who are most needy—often the lowest income students—while the differences generally decline as contributions, an indication of higher levels of wealth, increase.

Alternatively, a hybrid formula, which might represent the most politically viable approach, could be explored. Although Fischer dismisses this alternative as too complicated, various relatively straightforward approaches could be devised. For example, the results for particular subpopulations under the Pell Grant formula might justify using it for that subpopulation, while a modified CM might be selected for others. A case in point: there have been widespread complaints that the treatment of married students without children under CM requires too little contribution; Pell Grant results are seen as more realistic. Thus, Pell could be selected for that particular subpopulation. The most complex alternative, although not impossible to achieve, would involve alterations to a selected formula to produce acceptable results for all programs. In any event, failure to integrate the full formulas should not prohibit integration of existing or expanded versions of simplified formulas.

Nonetheless, Fischer's article has made a major contribution. Not only did Fischer stir debate, but he clearly demonstrated that integration is possible if one is willing to accept differential effects as the inevitable result. The challenge is to agree in advance on how to evaluate these results. Perhaps Fischer's most singular contribution is to show that the use of a single formula is mechanically feasible for Pell Grants by separating the calculation of contribution from the determination of award.

Assuming that these issues can be resolved successfully through the creation of a hybrid that reasonably mirrors the performance of the separate formulas, the benefits of integration are manifold and clear. First, a single formula would decrease the appearance of complexity for the applicants and the public at large and make the programs more understandable and accessible. Second, ironically, integration would deemphasize need analysis and increase emphasis on the role of the practitioner, as professionals would be called upon to deal with relatively unique classes of applicants who now are treated through separate formulas. Third, use of a single formula would substantially decrease regulatory burden by eliminating the rules necessary to control numerous systems. Finally, and perhaps most importantly, integration may actually constrain the political manipulation of the formula to control expenditures in a single program, that is, Pell Grants or Stafford Loans. Congress and the executive branch would be forced to resort to other methods than need analysis to achieve their goals. For example, a decision to impose or increase a deductible or a minimum contribution for Stafford Loans would have to be handled within program-specific rules (for example, regulations) because the same action would have negative implications for low-income Pell Grant recipients. Such a constraint would be healthy because it would maintain pressure to keep the formula (and therefore the application and general delivery process) relatively simple.

Streamlining Delivery

Simplification and integration would be great achievements, but they also pose daunting challenges. Streamlining the delivery process, particularly the application process, represents the most realistic opportunity to reduce complexity and burden in the student aid programs. Utilizing existing technology to move the delivery system from a paper-based to an electronic system is at the heart of streamlining delivery. While this transformation has been under way in parts of the delivery process for some time, reauthorization represents a unique opportunity to achieve significant enhancements by coordinating subtle program changes with technological advances in delivery.

The clearest example of the opportunities and benefits of streamlining can be observed in the area of reapplication. Currently, students apply for financial aid annually, and the Department of Education's processing systems create a new data base each year. Cross-year comparisons are conducted for analytical purposes only on the department's sample data base. This approach belies the fact that more than half of the student records in one year's data base are also present in the next. This fact raises the question of why applications are completed anew and data bases developed from scratch each year. Analyses have demonstrated that circumstances and individual data change substantially enough to justify filing annual applications. However, *updating* an existing application, from an existing data base, is both feasible and reasonable. Updating electronically rather than applying anew would substantially decrease applicant and institutional burden and minimize risk associated with many of the system start-up problems experienced in recent years. Characteristically, these problems have occurred with the application-processing subsystems and contractors rather than with the central data base.

Updating would further insulate the system from delays and potentially failure. New application requirements, such as default provisions, citizenship status, and registration for the draft, may require electronic matches with other data bases. Updating existing student records would eliminate the need for certain of these matches, once conducted, rather than duplicating them annually. Dispensing with such matches—and therefore the need for applicants to complete the questions on the application form—would eliminate some of the most frustrating aspects of delivery. In addition, verification requirements could be similarly affected. Once undergoing a thorough verification, a student's updated record could be subject to a minimal level of verification, as many items would change only incrementally.

Updating annual student aid applications electronically does raise issues related to data and management integrity. Some fear that updating would discourage applicants from altering existing data. However, the items that contribute most to changes in contributions and that are most likely to change substantially, such as number of family members in college, could be carefully scrutinized. Other procedures, including the requirement for signatures on key documents each time data are changed, would also have to be reevaluated. In an age in which billions of dollars are transferred daily by electronic means without the existence of documents and signatures, alternatives to current paper-based procedures must be considered. Of course, these alternatives must not diminish the fiscal and management integrity of the delivery system.

Reducing Regulations

Regulation designed to address key concerns, the most important of which threaten to undermine the existence of student aid programs, have been onerous and costly to many parties in the programs, particularly students and institutions. Deregulation has thus been discussed widely as a means of reducing the burden imposed by these regulations. Yet the problems associated with such issues as defaults have become so severe that deregulation is unlikely, perhaps unwise.

In an era in which Senate committees investigate fraud and abuse in the student aid programs and in the wake of the savings and loan debacle, deregulation has lost its appeal. Nevertheless, a new approach to regulating, largely untried in the student aid programs, deserves exploration. Performance-based regulation holds the promise of reducing the imposition of broad-scale regulatory burdens for problems that are found in only a portion of the students or institutions. It also implies the use of more management rather than procedural oversight.

Rather than specifying procedural verification requirements for all institutions, for example, institutions that demonstrate a high level of accuracy in awarding federal funds through comprehensive management and assessment procedures would be exempt from mandatory verification regulations. Currently, the Department of Education has a project in place that illustrates the effectiveness of such an approach. Institutions taking part in the project utilize quantitative and qualitative assessment procedures to evaluate their performance in delivering funds. Weaknesses are addressed through the implementation of corrective action plans. Although the institutions involved in the project are exempted from mandatory verification requirements, most maintain a high level of voluntary verification. But these procedures are tailored to their unique problems and are based on the measured effectiveness of the procedures in increasing the quality of data.

These principles can be applied to many areas of regulation; there is, in fact, much interest in extending the approach to default prevention. The principle as applied to default would apply certain regulations to institutions only when defaults exceed an acceptable level. For example, institutions with low default rates would not have to delay disbursement for certain borrowers for thirty days or have to use approved admissions tests for non–high school graduates attending the institution (whether they receive aid or not). High default-rate institutions would be required to impose such procedures.

Though performance-based regulation holds great promise, it also creates inequities and would require appropriate, defensible, and reliable performance measures. In part because of the regulatory approach currently used in student aid, policymakers are faced with a dearth of acceptable alternatives. Measures related to the quality of application data have been politicized by a decade of studies that were unpopular with the student aid community. Likewise, default rates have been the subject of many years of debate, and we await the repercussions of revoking institutional eligibility based on such calculations.

In addition, although the approach is logical on a practical level—not imposing requirements on institutions that do not have a problem—some will contend that performance-based regulations favor institutions with high levels of resources and middle-class students. Many private and large four-year public institutions will be exempted from regulation, whereas colleges with fewer resources serving lower income students (community colleges and smaller private and trade schools) will be subject to regulation. Measures that form the basis of performance-based regulation may be perceived as arbitrary and the associated burden as unfair in light of resources available and student served. But ultimately, performance-based regulation may be judged as superior to the current approach despite perceived inequity of the measures used.

Conclusion

The reauthorization process holds unprecedented promise for producing a significant reduction in both burden and complexity through simplification. Simplifying the need-analysis process facing students, by exempting some students and permitting more students to use the current simplified need analysis, represents great progress in this direction. Yet integrating the two existing formulas would result in still greater progress by producing a more understandable, less cumbersome system. Clearly, the task of integrating two complex formulas is daunting, but the difficulties involved should not be allowed to overcome the possibility for limited integration: creation of a single, expanded simplified formula.

Streamlining reapplication represents the greatest opportunity to simplify the process of awarding aid without creating other problems. Finally, the shift to performance-based regulation would free students and institutions from the burden of indiscriminate regulation. However, consensus regarding the performance indices must emerge, and the perceived inequities of the approach must be deemed an acceptable price.

Regardless of the success of the reauthorization process, realizing the full impact of these positive steps can be achieved only through the implementation process. Numerous parties have roles that will determine the degree of implementation. Institutions and states, for example, may ultimately determine the forms and processes to which students are subject. Unless these parties are committed to change, simplification will be illusory. However, in the wake of reauthorization, support for simplification alternatives may be so widespread that resistance to implementation of most alternatives may disappear.

References

Advanced Technology. *Title IV Quality Control Project: Corrective Actions*. Vol. 2. Reston, Va.: Advanced Technology, 1987.

Fischer, F. J. "Toward the Use of a Single Need Analysis." *Journal of Student Financial Aid,* 1990, *20* (2), 6–34.

Fitzgerald, B. K. "Equity and Efficiency: An Analysis of Simplifying the Pell Grant Eligibility Formula." Unpublished doctoral thesis, Graduate School of Education, Harvard University, 1990.

Price Waterhouse. *Integrated Quality Control Measurement Project: Findings and Corrective Actions.* Washington, D.C.: Price Waterhouse, 1990.

Brian K. Fitzgerald is staff director of the Advisory Committee on Student Financial Assistance.

The many changes that have taken place in the student aid system in recent years have necessitated a series of operational and programmatic adjustments for financial aid administrators and their offices.

Constant Response to Change: The Role of the Financial Aid Office

Natala K. Hart

The role of the financial aid administrator was established when the profession emerged in the early 1950s. The impetus leading to creation of the profession was a crisis of that time—institutions competing for a limited number of students by using institutional funds. This "bidding war" led to the formation in 1953 of a separate organization, the College Scholarship Service (CSS), which provided a framework for initial meetings of those first professional financial aid administrators; it was also at this time that members of the College Board and newly formed CSS enunciated a set of principles.

These principles (College Scholarship Service, 1989, p. 1.1), which served as the philosophical foundation for the profession and which still seem sound today, were the following:

1. The purpose of any financial aid program—institutional, governmental, or private—should be to provide monetary assistance to students who can benefit from further education but who cannot do so without such assistance. The primary purpose of a collegiate financial aid program should be to provide financial assistance to accepted students who, without such aid, would be unable to attend that college.
2. Each college has an obligation to assist in realizing the national goal of equality of educational opportunity. The college, therefore, should work with schools, community groups, and other educational institutions in support of this goal.
3. The college should publish budgets that state total student expenses realistically by including, where applicable, maintenance at home, commuting expenses, personal expenses, and necessary travel.

4. Parents are expected to contribute according to their means, taking into account their income, assets, number of dependents, and other relevant information. Students themselves are expected to contribute from their own assets and earnings, including appropriate borrowing against future earnings.
5. Financial aid should be offered only after determination that the resources of the family are insufficient to meet the student's educational expenses. The amount of aid offered should not exceed the amount needed to meet the difference between the student's total educational expenses and the family's resources.
6. The amount and type of self-help expected from students should be related to the circumstances of the individual. In the assignment of funds to those students designated to receive financial aid, the largest amounts of total grant assistance should go to students with the least ability to pay.
7. The college should review its financial assistance awards annually and adjust them, if necessary, to reflect changes in the financial needs of students and the expenses of attending the institution. The college has an obligation to inform students and parents of the financial aid renewal policies for enrolled students at the time of the initial offer of financial assistance.
8. Because the amount of financial assistance awarded reflects the economic circumstances of students and their families, the college should refrain from any public announcement of the amount of aid offered and encourage students, their secondary schools, and others to respect the confidentiality of this information.
9. All documents, correspondence, and conversations between and among aid applicants, their families, and financial aid officers are confidential and entitled to the protection ordinarily arising from a counseling relationship.
10. Concern for the student should be paramount. Financial aid should be administered in such a manner that other interests, important though they may be, are subordinate to the needs of students.

The profession initially focused on establishing student need. Because virtually no funds existed beyond institutional scholarship funds, the role of the financial aid administrator was to counsel students, to assess the cost of that student's attendance, and to evaluate the family's ability to meet that cost.

The students who came under scrutiny by the first financial aid administrators usually conformed to a particular type. Typically, that early student came from a two-parent, intact family with limited income and assets, entered college directly from high school, and rarely changed institutions before completing a degree.

The role of the financial aid administrator has changed rapidly and radically since those principles were enunciated. The common thread in these changes is the rapid expansion in available financial assistance that has occurred in the past forty years. Aid in the early 1950s was less than $100 million, was awarded to a few thousand students, and was available primarily from independent institutions' own resources. Today, more than $25 billion is awarded to over five million students, and the primary source is the federal government. Whether aid has been or is sufficient continues to be debated, but the expansion of the student aid programs unquestionably has increased access to postsecondary education, particularly for students from the nation's lowest income families. The added complexities in the role of the financial aid administrator are rooted directly in this monumental increase in funds requiring administration. Moreover, like the level and mix of financial aid funding, today's student recipient comes from much more diverse circumstances, a testimony to what happened when educational access was broadened.

Characteristics of Current Financial Aid Administrator Roles

The current slate of financial aid programs and the expanded number of eligible students shape the role of financial aid administrators. The following have emerged as key factors influencing this role: (1) large aid populations require a different approach to staff management than small aid populations, (2) cost of attendance—high, moderate, or low—influences aid administration, and (3) the availability of technological support fundamentally alters the process of financial aid determination and eligibility.

Nothing inherent in the financial aid programs causes these distinctions. They derive from the student populations served and the management responses to those populations. Nor are these distinctions sector-specific. For example, the functions of the financial aid administrator at a public institution serving a large out-of-state population often mirror those of independent college administrators.

The expansion in the number of students receiving financial aid has led to the growth in staff size. The early financial aid administrator was usually the only person on the campus conducting those duties; some offices now employ more than fifty people to complete financial aid processing and related activities. In addition, today's senior financial aid administrator deals with personnel policies, training, staff development, and other responsibilities associated with management of a large staff. Although these management functions are similar to those associated with any like-sized personnel group, the constant change of financial aid rules and procedures makes the training and staff-audit functions more demanding than in other management positions.

A student body seeking to meet high educational costs—whether at an independent institution or at a public university with a high percentage of out-of-state students—creates different demands than the student body at lower cost institutions. High cost necessarily entails offering a full array of federal and state programs, but it also increasingly dictates that significant institutional resources be devoted to student aid. Assuming standard composition within the student body, higher need not only leads to an additional number of students seeking aid, but also results in student applicants with more complex family circumstances than those attending lower cost institutions.

Administrators in higher cost environments typically must engage in institutional budget planning as well as in federal and state aid administration. Further, analyses of student need require delving into much more complex tax returns (those of businesses and corporations) and into issues involving assets, particularly home equity. It is important to emphasize again that these practices apply both to public and private institutions where students confront higher costs.

The financial aid functions at lower cost institutions are not necessarily easier. They simply are often different. At lower cost institutions a higher percentage of the students are likely to be self-supporting, have unique budgets (for example, child care costs), and also require frequent revision of their expected contribution from earnings.

Another factor differentiating positions within the profession is the level of automation of the student aid functions. Whether the staff is large or small, access to data processing support can significantly alter a campus's staff configuration and the associated management responsibilities of the financial aid administrator. Numerous demands for data changes, response to regulatory changes, and analysis of a campus's financial aid population require data processing. For large offices manual identification of the affected students and the inputting of changes would be virtually impossible; for small offices automation is similarly valuable. The need for automation is clear, but the intense demands for programming maintenance—necessitated by alterations in financial aid regulations and need-analysis rules—make automation a more difficult challenge for campuses than other systems applications. Systems usually have a lifetime of a few years before comprehensive modification is needed; financial aid systems usually change each year. The aid administrator must repeatedly petition for scarce data-processing resources to keep current with necessary changes.

The responsibility of the aid administrator on some campuses also has increasingly included a larger financial planning role, generally called "enrollment management." Analysis of fiscal demands for financial aid and the prediction of student choice under a series of financial aid packages and options are relatively new dimensions of the aid administrator's role.

Families now report that financial concerns loom above their concerns for admission to college. Financial aid has become vital to enrollment of students in the number and composition sought by a campus. Retention also relies on adequate financial aid. Thus, the inevitable conclusion is that a campus's enrollment—beyond those students affluent enough to pay full costs—is directly tied to available aid.

A final dimension of the financial aid matrix is the maturation of the profession itself. After thirty years of fulfilling a distinct set of responsibilities, the first cohort of aid administrators is retiring, and the profession has reshaped itself to meet new administrative demands. That reshaping is due in part to greater student reliance on loans, which requires an additional set of interactions with lenders and guarantors of student loans and a more complex set of counseling duties for students incurring potentially significant levels of indebtedness. Expansion of the loan programs has also brought about a complex and changing set of regulatory requirements, which will be explored more fully later in this chapter.

The profession is also being reshaped because of the growing gap between families' ability to pay and the cost of college, a development that creates demand for new financing options and increases the need for information about college savings and financing. All these forces produce job requirements quite different from the counseling-based focus of the first student aid professionals.

Reasons for Changing Administrative Demands

Three primary factors have contributed to changes in the administrative demands placed on the financial aid professional. First is the increased availability of financial aid and the expansion of its sources. Second is the greater complexity of the family circumstances of students served by financial aid, and third is the increased regulation resulting from the provision of more and more public funds.

The sizable increase in student aid over the thirty-plus year history of the profession has, as earlier noted, come primarily from the expansion of public sector involvement. The federal role in providing student aid is now dominant, the states' roles secondary. On a national level, institutions rank third in aid provided to students. (This ranking does not include lenders, who provide very significant amounts of their capital but who are also compensated for those funds.) More aid from outside sources means that student aid administrators must concern themselves more often with forces outside the institution, the providers of public funds, than was once the case.

These changes in the source of funds distinguish the independent institution's aid administrator from that of the public institution. At independent institutions significant amounts of funds come from their own resources. At public institutions, federal and state aid sources exceed those of the institution. However, even for independent schools, the importance of maintaining levels of federal and state assistance is critical and makes the administrator's role one that appears to concentrate on external concerns.

Responding to the demands of federal and state financial aid regulations and keeping apace of those changes also force today's institutional aid administrator to direct energies to functions outside the institution. Although the importance to the institution of sustaining the delivery of outside funds is clear, the role of the aid administrator within the campus environment often appears ambiguous. Coupled with the highly technical detail of student aid administration, this phenomenon leads to a perception that the financial aid administrator's orientation lies outside the institution and is possibly in conflict with perceived or real institutional needs. Within the aid office the counseling role and the need-analysis function have become more complicated because of changes in relationships within families and of more limited family ability to finance a college education. Formerly, as we have noted, dealing with a student other than one from a two-parent family was once rare for aid administrators. Today, more than half of the nation's aid recipients are self-supporting—reliant on their own, rather than their parents', financial resources. These students have more variable incomes, often have left full-time employment to return to college, and are part of more complex family structures than the dependent student. This situation produces individualized costs of attending college.

Similarly, in the time the profession has existed, the nation's family structure has also changed. With greater prevalence of divorce, remarriage, and the blending of families, determining who has responsibility to pay for college has become more complicated. The aid administrator often must deal with very different sets of family expectations and financial practices, and these factors create difficult and emotion-laden discussions. Matters of confidentiality and information acquisition and release are more complex.

Finally, the information-analysis role of the aid administrator is becoming more difficult as higher income families with more complex financial situations enter the student aid recipient pool. Sorting out true need between students of equal levels of adjusted gross income is a major new responsibility of today's aid administrator. In an attempt to provide more accurate and verifiable data for the student aid need-analysis process, aid forms contain references to comparable lines on the Internal Revenue tax forms. The tie between the financial aid process and the Internal Revenue tax structure may assure accurate data, but it also masks major distinctions between students. Reductions in income are sometimes appropriate for assessment of taxes but do not reflect a reduced ability to pay for college. For example, a family with $15,000 of earned income differs greatly in its ability to pay for college from a family with a business or corporation that legitimately writes off income for tax purposes. The aid administrator needs more financial and tax knowledge than did previous professionals in order to assess correctly available resources.

Aid administrators also respond to added demands of regulation by federal and to a lesser degree by state aid providers. Expansion of aid from public sources has brought growing public scrutiny. Aid is now a major federal expenditure. Concern about appropriate expenditure of funds has predictably increased dramatically. Oversight has intensified, as evidence of misuse of funds has surfaced, as reductions in aid available to middle-income families has reduced their support for aid programs, and as more dollars generate increased demand for accountability.

Many financial aid administrators contend that regulations, though burdensome, would be less so if they were not changed so often (sometimes retroactively) and were focused more specifically on those institutions that should change. A master calendar was instituted by Congress to stabilize changes in the student aid system; Congress mandated that changes be final on December 1 of the year prior to the applicable academic year. Yet the requirement to input revisions to regulations and demands to decrease federal expenditures have meant that regulations constantly fluctuate. Identifying affected students and implementing changes, often with major computer-system reprogramming, has frustrated aid administrators.

The monolithic nature of regulations intended to control abuse or mismanagement of aid has been even more frustrating for student aid administrators. Acknowledged need for change at some point in the student aid delivery process has often led to changes imposed on all institutions, even those with demonstrated success in the regulated areas. In this era of limited resources already stretched to their limits by expansion of student aid, the price of enforcing regulations that produce no results at institutions with demonstrated good practices has involved more than money and aggravation. It has led to less time for student counseling, information dissemination, and other more productive functions sorely needed by students and the institutions themselves.

Recent examples of attempts to regulate institutions have come through the Stafford Loan Program. Regulatory efforts to diminish expenditures in the program have been aimed primarily at defaults and at addressing needless defaults, especially those created through institutions' abuse of the program. Although virtually all aid administrators agree that measures toward this end are appropriate, they also note that some significant expansion of defaults has been created as students from lower income backgrounds have borrowed more and more from the loan programs. Because these lower income students have a higher probability of default, some increases are predictable. Thus, the fundamental dilemma is to distinguish abuse from these predictable instances while trying to reduce overall default rates and assuring that defaulting on a student loan remains clearly unacceptable and bears appropriately high penalties.

Future Directions in the Role of the Student Aid Administrator

The context of the many difficult changes in the role of the aid administrator over the past three decades has been obscured in some circles. As we have seen, greater responsibilities are the result of massive expansion of the student aid programs, which secured a greater level of access to higher education than would otherwise have ever been possible. Larger programs have also brought about major growth in the number of financial aid positions; additionally, the role of aid administrators has become more diverse along with the student bodies they serve, and with diversity has come frustration. Given these changes, the obvious question arises: What is the future likely to hold, and how will higher education administration respond?

The demand for financial aid certainly will continue to grow. There is no indication that college costs will drop below increases in family income at any point in the future. The aid administrator will need not only to assist families in meeting those costs, but also to encourage families to save for college expenses. Skills in financial planning and long-term investment will therefore clearly be required.

Automation will also assume greater importance in the management of financial aid. The array of student aid programs and their attendant rules will require even more technological skill to keep pace with change, even in the smallest office. The technological component of the aid administrator's job will also affect staffing patterns in the financial aid office. As existing aid administrators in entry positions become proficient with technology, learn to cope with high stress and equally high work volumes, and develop analytic skills, many will leave the profession for more lucrative positions. This pattern is already in evidence as positions one step from the top are more and more difficult to fill.

Future aid administrators will turn an increasing portion of their attention back to the campus. With public funds levelling off, more institutional dollars will fill the gap. Aid administrators will thus be pressed for time and analysis for institutional planning even though federal and state demands will not decrease.

Discussions about changes in student aid regulation are likely to result in a set of performance standards that will eliminate unproductive regulation of campuses with demonstrated success in student aid administration. The incentives for self-regulation are clear: institutions would be able to avoid changes in areas where revised practices would not likely produce improved results.

Future aid administrators will be challenged to deal with more funds and a wider variety of students. New funds are not likely to be fully adequate but will attempt to meet broader national purposes, especially future manpower and training requirements. Older students, students of less traditional academic type, and those with less academic preparation will present themselves to campuses and for financial assistance.

All of these are the demands that society will certainly place on higher education and to which both higher education and the nation itself must respond.

Reference

College Scholarship Service. *Manual for Student Aid Administrators, 1990–91 Policies and Procedures.* New York: College Entrance Examination Board, 1989.

Natala K. Hart is executive director of the Indiana Student Assistance Commission.

Financial aid is one of several variables that policymakers must consider in any effort to improve college persistence.

Where Do We Go from Here: Looking Beyond Student Aid and Access to Persistence

Oscar F. Porter

The previous essays in this journal focus on topics such as the history and rationale of student aid, the partners who share the responsibility to provide it, the mechanics that determine the involvement and commitment of those partners, and suggestions for refinement or wholesale change of the existing delivery system. This final chapter is intended to use those earlier discussions as a point of departure to consider a different facet of student aid—its role in affecting a college student's persistence in completing an undergraduate program.

Let me clarify the perspective of this essay in the context of what McPherson (1988) defines as the three purposes of federal student aid: equal educational opportunity, fairer sharing of college costs, and more stable institutional financial security. First, equal educational opportunity is defined to include persistence and degree completion, not simply the chance to go to college. Second, the sources of aid we consider will go beyond the federal government to include the institution, parents, corporate, and foundation sources. Therefore, who bears the cost of college and how that cost should be distributed will be addressed. Finally, this discus-

---

The views in this chapter represent those of the author. They should not be construed as the position of the National Institute of Independent Colleges and Universities, the National Association of Independent Colleges and Universities, or any of their member institutions.

sion will be concerned with undergraduate students and their financial security, not with the financial interests of the institutions they attend.

Concentration thus far on access to college and opportunity for college choice as the main concern has taken the interests of students only as far as the beginning of their educational journey. Much of the earlier discussion has led us through the byzantine world the student faces in finding the appropriate mix of information and resources to begin college. The unexplored question is, "Does student aid exert an influence over persistence and degree completion?" What follows is a response to that question. It is based on the research literature on student financial aid but also relies on the prudent application of the oldest and most common of all methodologies—speculation.

With reauthorization of the Higher Education Act looming before us this year and the changes that this legislation forebodes, what we know now about the influences of student aid is likely to lose some of its relevance. Just what the new strategies will be is anyone's guess. Proposals fly fast and furiously. If grants are weighted in favor of the first two years, will not students be more likely to complete a program or degree? Is redistributing tuition as institutional aid the best way for colleges and universities to support low-income and underrepresented student populations? Would allowing everyone to borrow the price of college from a national trust fund and repay it over a working lifetime be the most equitable way to finance postsecondary education? Could the College Work-Study program be restructured to provide more meaningful experiences for students through public or community service opportunities off campus? None of these ideas is new, nor is this list of them exhaustive. The point they have in common is that their effects are unknown and can only be speculated about.

Research on Student Aid and Persistence

What do we know about student aid and its effects on student persistence and degree completion? The answer to this question depends on the assumptions made about the effects that student aid should have. There seem to be two broad approaches to understanding the impact of aid. First, there is the approach based on the question of whether or not a particular type of aid or aid package is more conducive to persistence. The second broad approach is concerned with whether or not aid produces educational equity by removing the effects of income differences.

These two approaches are not mutually exclusive, and research on the broad effectiveness of student aid is often presented along with analysis by types of aid. It is important to remember, however, that the underlying assumptions of the approaches are different. The first assumes that student aid does function to equalize educational opportunity and is therefore concerned with discovering what kind of aid is associated with better persistence and performance. The other makes no assumptions about the effectiveness of student aid and endeavors to establish the basic effect assumed in the first research approach.

The approach focusing on the influence of types of aid appeared first, perhaps because it grew out of the study of college students, not primarily out of policy research. The work of A. W. Astin, beginning in the late 1960s and early 1970s, appears to be the work that is most often cited, replicated, refined, or refuted. His findings over the years indicate that grants and work-study are beneficial for student persistence but loans are not. This situation is especially true for those groups expected to be most influenced by student aid—low-income and underrepresented minority students (A. W. Astin, 1975 and 1982; H. Astin and Cross, 1981). In a major study of minority students in American higher education, A. W. Astin reported that loans are harmful to minority student persistence. This corroboration of earlier findings came at a crucial time as loans began to supersede grants as a source of student aid in the late 1970s.

The results of subsequent research, however, have not been as clear cut. Several studies have found a positive influence for grants and scholarships (Pantages and Creedon, 1978; Jensen, 1981), but others have not (Peng and Fetters, 1978). Also, qualifications have been made about the positive effect of scholarships and grants, such as the necessity for a minimum amount of grant before the effect appears ($2,250 in Carroll, 1987) or the need for long-term availability of grant and scholarship support through mechanisms like renewable scholarships (Woodward, 1988).

As for other aid sources, the evidence is sometimes limited and occasionally mixed, too. The majority of data on loans supports a negative effect, but there are also findings of no effects, either positive or negative. The recent work of Mortenson and Wu (1990) indicates that concern about taking on loans in significant amounts influences both entry and persistence of minority and low-income students. There is very little information on college work-study or self-help, but what there is supports the positive influence of this type of aid (A. W. Astin, 1975; H. Astin and Cross, 1981; Olivas, 1986; Tinto, 1987; J. Porter, Gregory, and Fenske, 1990).

The one area not mentioned thus far is parental and family support. In his earliest work A. W. Astin found that students whose parents furnish their primary source of financial support had a higher likelihood of graduating than lower socioeconomic-status students who relied on aid (Astin, 1975). The most recent reports on rising college costs from the U.S. Department of Education indicate that the burden of paying for college has fallen more on the shoulders of students and parents in recent years as other sources of support (especially federal grant support) have not kept up with increasing tuitions in all types of institutions (U.S. Department of Education, 1990). Another recent study found that family financial support was positively and directly related to the number of months a student spends in a four-year college or university (O. F. Porter, 1990b).

Overall, the studies on effects of different student aid types would lead us to believe that grants are probably the most effective source of aid for persistence, especially if they are renewable throughout the years of study and provide significant amounts of money. Work-study or self-help support has considerable potential to enhance persistence as well. Loans, especially in large amounts or as the single source of student aid, are more likely to have a negative effect on persistence than other types of support. Finally, the role of parental or family financial support appears to be growing in importance as other sources of aid provide a smaller proportion of student need.

All of these findings, however, are based on comparisons of the performance of students receiving some form of student aid. There is an implicit assumption that aid has a positive effect. This brings us to the second approach to student aid and persistence research: comparison of students who receive aid with those who do not to examine the general effect of aid on persistence. Prior to the 1980s, there was a lack of longitudinal or national data bases that described distribution of aid and packaging, no information on need-based versus nonneed-based aid, and limited theoretical foundations for assessing the effects of student aid (Stampen and Fenske, 1988). In other words, one could not be sure that the findings about specific types of aid applied to the larger question of whether aid assists persistence.

Some partial answers can be found in the earlier approach to student aid research. Voorhees (1985) found that all forms of campus-based aid showed a positive effect on persistence. Terkla (1984) found that financial aid was the third strongest influence on persistence in her study, which took into account socioeconomic status. Nevertheless, nagging doubts persisted because of findings such as those by Peng and Fetters (1978), who found a negligible relationship between financial aid and withdrawal from college.

One of the problems with earlier work was the lack of data about the same people over time. Do the same people get aid throughout their college years? Are the amounts the same? Are the packages the same? Without some information on these basic questions, one cannot make valid comparisons.

In recent years the work of Stampen and Cabrera has shed considerable light on these questions regarding student aid and persistence. They found that the aid recipient population remained fairly stable over time, but rarely was aid received in the same form from year to year. However, students who received grants were more likely to continue to receive grants, and students who received loans were more likely to receive loans throughout their undergraduate careers. They also concluded that need-based student aid was essential to the persistence of low-income students (Stampen and Cabrera, 1986).

The most important result of their research came in a followup study. They found that there was no difference between the persistence of aided and nonaided students. Therefore, it appeared that aid eliminated the financial difficulties that might have been a cause of leaving college (Stampen and Cabrera, 1988). Educational opportunity was equal, a fact that could be attributed to the availability of aid. Additional support for this belief is found in a meta-analysis of thirty research studies on persistence (Murdock, 1987). It was found that the presence of financial aid reduced the risk of dropout among low-income students to nearly the same levels as those of middle-income and high-income students.

Thus, a body of evidence suggests that student aid, in general, has a positive effect on student persistence and that various types and combinations of aid can enhance that general effect. Manipulating the student aid system to increase grant assistance, to provide more work-study and self-help support, and to minimize the use of loans as the sole or major source of aid has the potential to increase student persistence and, ultimately, degree completions.

A Policy Dilemma

No outcome in social science research, however, is ever this simple. Policymakers want *the* answer, but research may only provide a variety of options. Some options are clearly better than others, but each comes with its own list of caveats that could significantly affect the outcomes of any policy based on that option.

Perhaps the dilemma for policymakers who wish to use student aid to expand the definition of equal access to include persistence and degree completion is best expressed by juxtaposing our conclusions thus far with the following quote: "Although finances are very commonly cited by both researchers and withdrawing students alike as an important reason for leaving, there is little direct evidence to support the claim that finances are, in and of themselves, significant determinants of student departure" (Tinto, 1987, p. 80).

Tinto agrees with other research (for example, Jackson, 1978; Tierney, 1980) indicating that much of the impact of finances on persistence occurs at entry; financial considerations influence whether to attend and where to enroll. He also comments that aid has a marginal effect on the decision to leave school for most students (except those who are truly low-income) and that the cost/benefit of dropping out may play a more important part in the decision to leave. "Finances do not appear to be a long-term factor in persistence" (Tinto, 1987, p. 82).

Having successfully identified some actions that could be taken to improve persistence, must policymakers now abandon them in the face of this statement by one of the foremost researchers in the field? Are the proposals not valid after all? The answer is yes and no. What all this may mean is not that they are without value, but that there are more factors, as yet unidentified, with sufficient influence on persistence to offset the importance of student aid as described in the earlier research.

Other Influences on Persistence

If financial aid is not *the* principal factor in student persistence, what are the other influences, and how do they compare with student aid? Some of them should not surprise anyone. Good high school grades and admissions tests have long been associated with college performance, persistence, and completion (A. W. Astin, 1975; Demitroff, 1974; Nettles, 1984; Mingle, 1987). In fact, Stampen and Cabrera (1986) found that academic performance in high school was the single most powerful predictor of persistence.

Another key variable is socioeconomic status or one of its components, such as parental education or family income (Mingle, 1987; Carroll, 1987; Durán, 1986; Mestre, 1986; Peng, 1977). In his review of the literature, Wolfle (1983) reports that high socioeconomic status and prior educational attainment are the strongest predictors of postsecondary attainment.

The other major area of influence on persistence is the college environment itself, or the student's experience in that environment. Specific variables associated with persistence include institutional quality (Cope and Hannah, 1975), size (A. W. Astin, 1975; Tinto, 1987), interaction with faculty (Tinto, 1975 and 1987; Pantages and Creedon, 1978; A. W. Astin, 1975 and 1985), and advising and counseling (Lenning, Sauer, and Beal, 1980; Coulson and others, 1981). In addition, preparation and course work in high school (Malcom, 1985; Christoffel, 1986) and student aspirations (Trent and Medsker, 1968; Peng, 1977; Mingle, 1987) appear to have significant effects.

The influence of factors other than student aid is also important in understanding the persistence of specific groups for whom student aid programs were intended—low-income and minority students. These factors take on even more importance in the context of Stampen and Fenske's warning that "research on student financial aid is not very illuminating about low-income and minority students' access and persistence" (Stampen and Fenske, 1988, p. 342).

Just what are some of these variables? Muñoz (1986) found that stress plays a particularly important role in the persistence of Chicano students. The lack of student aid that is guaranteed from year to year and the prospect of high indebtedness from student loans are clear sources of anxiety for the students. Nevertheless, receiving aid does not reduce the stress felt by Chicano students. In fact, Muñoz found that across all institutional types and aid packages, Chicano students reported more stress in their lives than did Anglo students.

Olivas (1986) cautions that generational differences (particularly, whether parents have attended college) in the Latino community can have a direct influence on enrollment and persistence. It is likely that similar comments could be made about other first-generation college students, too. For many college students, parents recognize that the child's obligations to family and to work may have to be reduced. However, first-generation college students, especially minority students, can expect less understanding. There is a body of research indicating that obligations to family and to work influence persistence and completion for minority students even more than for the average undergraduate (Chacón, Cohen, and Strover, 1986; Durán, 1986; A. W. Astin, 1977 and 1982).

In their evaluation of the Special Services for Disadvantaged Students program, Coulson and others (1981) found that minority students whose parents earned higher incomes were at reduced risk at all types of institutions (as demonstrated by higher grades, higher persistence rates, and more normal progress to degree completion) than students from lower income backgrounds. Although Coulson and others did find a similar pattern among students who received large amounts of student aid, it appeared that availability to and use of compensatory services were as important as the aid itself.

In their recent monograph on high-risk students in higher education, Jones and Watson (1990) propose three components for any retention program: a demonstrated commitment to the student that is both financial and personalized, a monitoring system for at-risk students, and social as well as academic support. This approach is holistic, and it requires the institution to share the responsibility for success with the student.

Perhaps a return to the work of Tinto will bring this part of the discussion full circle. It is his contention that attributing a student's decision to leave college to financial distress is a "polite" way of indicating problems with the student's social or intellectual life at the college or university. He says, "For most students, persistence is more reflective of the character of their social and intellectual experiences on campus than it is of their financial resources" (Tinto, 1987, p. 158). The individual's response to financial problems is conditioned by these other forces; those who are already stretched to the limit financially will experience these forces more strongly.

The Context for Policy

Let us return again to the position of the policymaker. The circumstances influencing persistence are less mysterious than they once were. There is now evidence to indicate that student financial aid can improve student persistence, but not entirely by itself. There are other factors—the student's background, academic preparation, ethnic/racial/cultural experience, generational status, aspirations, and college experience—that have direct and indirect influences on persistence. Clearly, some courses of action are more practicable, as well as more effective, than others. However, no single policymaker or group has access to all the possibilities.

What this policy environment suggests is not that one set of policymakers could or should control all the elements essential to student persistence. However, any policymaker can benefit from a fuller understanding of the variety of factors and their relationships to each other. The greater the number of policy decisions that can be made in the context of a common understanding of the phenomenon of persistence—and in sufficient concert to maximize the positive effects of those decisions—the more likely that progress can be made toward the desired outcome: true opportunity for all students.

But, of course, policymakers can not be referred to in any monolithic sense. It is time to identify the specific sources of policy and offer some suggestions about using those courses of action they can control to determine the future of higher education. For that purpose, the policy arenas to be discussed are the federal government (the administration and Congress), the state government, the institution, and the corporate and foundation community.

Underlying all of the discussion to come is a basic assumption that access means entry into postsecondary education *and* exit from it with a degree or other form of program completion. For good reason the focus of much student aid policy has been on paving the way for students to go to college and on giving them an opportunity to select the institution best suited to their needs. Now we must turn to the issue of outcomes of college attendance. Unless the students who make their way into our colleges and universities with the support of student aid persist and complete their programs, all efforts for access and equity are hollow. The research indicates quite clearly that low-income and minority students do not persist and complete at the same rate as students from the Anglo community or more affluent backgrounds (for example, O. F. Porter, 1990a). Therefore, our focus is on what policymakers can do to develop support for equitable outcomes.

Action in the Policy Arenas

The Federal Scene. With its reauthorization on everyone's mind at the federal policy level, the Higher Education Act is perhaps the best place to start. Our current system of grants and loans worked reasonably well to enhance entry until the last decade. In the 1980s, however, loans overtook grants as the principal means of federal support; Social Security benefits were lost; loan indebtedness became a concern for students both at entry and after leaving higher education; loan defaults dominated policy discussions in the last years of the decade; and tuition increases outpaced inflation and increases in grant aid. These changes came at a time when higher education enrollments became more diverse in terms of socioeconomic background, age, racial and ethnic background, and number of courses being taken; when students took longer to complete the traditional two-year and four-year degrees than in the past; when completion rates overall were lower; and when the greatest growth in federal student aid was seen in the for-profit proprietary sector.

If the federal effort is to be restructured with student persistence in mind, what should be done? To begin with, the balance between grant and loan support should be shifted back toward the grant side. As we have seen, one of the more consistent findings in the persistence literature concerning student aid is the positive effect of grants as opposed to loans.

One of the major proposals under consideration at the federal level is the restructuring of the Pell Grant program to concentrate all its resources on the critical first two years of college. The amount of the maximum grant would be increased dramatically, and the program would become an entitlement. After these first two years, students would have to rely on loans, institutional aid, and other resources for their financial support.

Yet "front-loading" all grant support into the first two years is not necessarily the answer. The answer for systematic support throughout the undergraduate years, coupled with the student's assurance that such support will be available each year, has already been discussed in the review of the persistence literature.

Of course, front-loading grants would reduce the likelihood that students who withdrew or finished a program in the first two years would incur substantial debt. However, it also guarantees that students with financial need who go on to complete a four-year degree (which now takes the average student closer to six years) will still face significant, possibly increased, debt. The idea that students who have committed themselves for the first two years will be more willing to accept large loans to finish what they have started is speculative at best.

The research of Mortenson and Wu (1990) strongly indicates that for low-income families the expectation of substantial debt is enough to keep students from opting for college at all. Front-loading does not address this concern in the long term. Whether the debt comes early or late is not important; its simple existence is enough. Implicit in the front-loading approach is a "bait and switch" mentality that is at best condescending, surely naive, and might even be cynical. The loan burdens of students will be reduced only if they choose not to continue. This is certainly not the message that federal policy should be sending to low-income, first-generation, and minority college students.

There are aspects of the front-loading approach that could be adapted to have a positive influence on persistence. Greater amounts of grant and lower amounts of loan at the beginning of a student's college career could indeed reduce the debt potential of students who leave early. The ratio of loan and grant support could be adjusted throughout the undergraduate years without completely eliminating grant support in the later years.

At the federal student aid program level, perhaps the key to effective support for persistence will come from one of the more underutilized programs—College Work-Study (CWS). On many campuses CWS is used to fill out the student's package after grants and loans have been awarded. If Tinto's and A. W. Astin's belief that integration and campus involvement are keys to persistence, work-study and self-help efforts on campus should receive greater prominence. The assumption here is that the greater the number of connections students have to the campus, the more likely they are to become part of that community, adopt its values, and transfer loyalties from other competing environments that decrease the likelihood of persistence.

Of course, increasing the prominence of College Work-Study will require additional appropriations by Congress (and by institutions from their own budgets), but so will front-loading grants and increasing their maximum amounts. There is little, if anything, in the literature on persistence that indicates an effect of grants beyond their role in financial support. Yet the literature is rife with reports about the importance of the first year or two to completion of a degree and the necessity of a personal connection between the student and the institution to increase persistence. Employing College Work-Study as a major component of student aid in the first two years is at least as likely as front-loading grants to enhance persistence. In combination with grant support that is guaranteed to continue throughout the undergraduate years, the effect of CWS on persistence should be significant. Loans are now an accepted part of the federal approach and should be continued, but as part of packaging that begins with family contribution, grant, and College Work-Study, not as the principal source of support in the later years of undergraduate study.

There is also another role for the federal government that should be expanded. The policy levers that are not attached directly to student financial aid but can affect persistence must be pulled in coordination with student aid efforts. In particular, support for the TRIO programs, and especially Student Support Services, needs to receive greater emphasis. Even students who receive financial aid require other compensatory services.

Among the TRIO programs Support Services receives the least attention in policy making and the fewest appropriations. The failure to utilize Support Services is unfortunate, as it not only provides personal and academic counseling, but also manifests in a very tangible way the ongoing concern of the federal government in the progress of the student. Direct financial support for students is essential, but indirect assistance through the development of a campus safety net is just as critical, especially for persistence and degree completion. Additional support and expansion of programs available under Support Services would constitute a federal policy that would be cost-effective, and generally beneficial, in furthering the aspirations of students who are receiving federal financial aid.

As students enter the final years of their degree programs, the opportunity to work in the fields they are studying as careers plays a role in their determination to complete their programs. Here again, the federal government could assist by increasing support for cooperative education and extended internships. Using a model that requires student and/or institutional matching support, a policy to provide real world experience would make the connection between the classroom and the work place and help those students who are making an economic cost/benefit decision about whether to continue their undergraduate programs. The federal policy would be supporting another aspect of the college experience associated with persistence while reinforcing the traditional partnership for college financing that requires commitments from students and institutions alike.

The State Scene. At the state level there are two broad policy areas influencing student persistence that are under state control: precollegiate preparation and the financing approach of the public higher education system. In the first area the states are making efforts to improve the quality and content of elementary and secondary education. Nevertheless, there are still a large number of students who go on to college without sufficient or appropriate preparation. According to Mortenson (1990), fewer than half of the students who took their examination had completed the federally recommended core high school curriculum. Not surprisingly, students from low-income and historically underrepresented groups were the least well prepared. It is the high dropout rates in these groups that leads many to question the effectiveness of student aid programs.

The country is experiencing difficult financial times, a fact illustrated only too well by the large number of state budgets in deficit. Public higher education must manage its resources even more effectively than in the past. Over the past few years there has been a shift in enrollment by upper-middle-income and wealthy students away from independent institutions to the public system (Mortenson and Wu, 1990; National Association of Independent Colleges and Universities, 1989). With the tuition subsidy all students receive (regardless of financial need) at public colleges and universities, this seems like a shrewd move on the part of upper-income families.

Shrewd it may be, but does the subsidy serve the purposes of equity and opportunity? Tuition and fees are not affected by income in public institutions; thus, the subsidy is less necessary for some than others. Granted, the assumption underlying the practice is that taxpayers are supporting public higher education according to the level of their tax payments. Some are already paying more than others. Yet although that assumption may once have been true, the tax revolution of the last decade seems to have done more to relieve the burdens of the wealthy than the poor. This fact calls into question a single state tuition rate.

The introduction of public tuitions based on income would serve two purposes. There would be a more equitable payment for services received by students, and the states would have more flexibility in their higher education budgets in these difficult times. The uses of those newly freed funds are myriad. Some could be recycled to the neediest students to cut down on their loan, or subsequent debt, burden. Some could be used to provide matching funds for federal College Work-Study to increase awards or broaden the recipient pool. State programs modeled on federal support services would certainly enhance the effectiveness of federal and institutionally supported efforts. Funds could be shifted into a pool from which grants or allocations might be made to those institutions, both public and independent, with effective programs to enhance persistence. In fact, applying the funds to efforts to increase or maintain institutional quality (faculty lines, facilities, etc.) could also have a positive effect on student persistence and performance.

Granted, the money under discussion here may be more a hope than a reality in tight budgetary times. Some may object to redistribution of wealth by the government. Yet the actions suggested here appear to be capable of directly effecting a result desired by states—increased college completion by their residents.

Perhaps the efforts in the states could be enhanced by the development of partnerships with the federal government. The State Student Incentive Grant program (SSIG) might provide one model for a cooperative effort. Similar approaches using federal funding to leverage state matching resources could be used to support persistence programs employing activities modeled on TRIO strategies.

The Campus Scene. Higher education institutions, especially those in the independent sector, also play a crucial role in providing student aid support. A recent report on institutional aid in independent colleges and universities found that nearly 80 percent of that aid is need-based and that some of the aid awarded under merit-based programs takes need into account, too (National Institute of Independent Colleges and Universities, 1990). What is not clear is how much of that support goes to the very neediest students in either public or independent institutions. By tailoring their grants carefully, institutions could use their support to best effect in support of persistence. Also, the commitment of funds over the period of the degree program—to provide renewable support rather than an enrollment lure—will further enhance that effectiveness. Finally, students participating in campus support services programs could be targeted to receive significant institutional grant support in place of loans in their student aid packages.

Much of the student support activity that influences persistence positively originates with the institution and is supported by its funds. The outcomes of these efforts should be evaluated and their successes publicized. Budget supplements for successful programs and matching funds to leverage governmental and private resources should be made available. Colleges and universities must remember that lack of initial program success should not result in the abandonment of the effort to change and improve. The failure of an approach should be examined, and new efforts based on that assessment should be initiated.

In addition to the genuine concern that institutions have for their students, they have another reason to support retention and persistence programming. Every student who stays another semester or another year is one who does not have to be replaced by the marketing and recruiting office. Every student who graduates is a potential donor, and graduates who have received support are more likely to feel positive about the institution and programs that led to their personal success.

The Corporate and Foundation Scene. Corporations and foundations that support higher education also have a role to play in efforts to enhance persistence. Their donations could assist effective persistence strategies ranging from scholarships, to support services, to internships and cooperative education opportunities. Having a building with a corporate or foundation name on it may have more appeal but less merit than subsidizing the hiring of support services counselors, initiating a new tutorial or mentoring program, or providing funds so that the neediest students can make ends meet without taking on an additional job. In all these efforts, the role of the corporate or foundation sponsor could be used to extract additional commitments from the traditional student aid partners. Rewarding initiative should come easily to those who place a premium on success in the marketplace.

Conclusion

The suggestions offered here may not be new or particularly innovative, but they may be useful nevertheless. The organizing theme behind this discussion has been that student aid is but one way to increase the desired outcome of attending college—finishing the program. Persistence is an accumulative, multivariate process, and no policymaker can influence all the variables. Each, however, can understand them and can know who has access to the others. In this way policy may be coordinated to enhance the effects of the different approaches that are being selected.

Student aid policy can influence student persistence, but the best effect will be generated if that policy can be made part of a holistic, multifaceted approach. If such a perspective can be adopted, we will spend less time worrying about why student aid has failed to expand access, participation, and persistence. Then we can concentrate on developing an integrated, broadly representative policy that recognizes the multidimensional character of students as individual people who are engaged in the undergraduate experience.

References

Astin, A. W. *Preventing Students from Dropping Out.* San Francisco: Jossey-Bass, 1975.

Astin, A. W. *Four Critical Years: Effects of College on Beliefs, Attitudes, and Knowledge.* San Francisco: Jossey-Bass, 1977.

Astin, A. W. *Minorities in American Higher Education: Recent Trends, Current Prospects, and Recommendations.* San Francisco: Jossey-Bass, 1982.

Astin, A. W. *Achieving Academic Excellence: A Critical Assessment of Priorities and Practices in Higher Education.* San Francisco: Jossey-Bass, 1985.

Astin, H., and Cross, P. "Black Students in White Institutions." In G. E. Thomas (ed.), *Black Students in Higher Education in the 1970s.* Westport, Conn.: Greenwood Press, 1981.

Carroll, D. *The Effects of Grants on College Persistence.* Washington, D.C.: National Center for Education Statistics, 1987.

Chacón, M., Cohen, E., and Strover, S. "Chicanas and Chicanos: Barriers to Progress in Higher Education." In M. Olivas (ed.), *Latino College Students.* New York: Teachers College Press, 1986.

Christoffel, P. "Minority Student Access and Retention: A Review." *Research and Development Update.* New York: College Board, 1986.

Cope, R., and Hannah, W. *Revolving College Doors: The Causes and Consequences of Dropping Out, Stopping Out, and Transferring.* New York: Wiley, 1975.

Coulson, J. E., and others. *Evaluation of the Special Services for Disadvantaged Students Program: 1979–80 Academic Year.* Santa Monica, Calif.: Systems Development Corporation, 1981.

Demitroff, J. F. "Student Persistence." *College and University,* 1974, *49,* 553–567.

Durán, R. P. "Prediction of Hispanics' College Achievement." In M. Olivas (ed.), *Latino College Students.* New York: Teachers College Press, 1986.

Jackson, G. A. "Financial Aid and Student Enrollment." *Journal of Higher Education,* 1978, *49,* 548–574.

Jensen, E. L. "Student Financial Aid and Persistence in College." *Journal of Higher Education,* 1981, *52* (3), 280–294.

Jones, D. J., and Watson, B. C. *"High Risk" Students in Higher Education: Future Trends.* ASHE-ERIC Higher Education Report, no. 3. Washington, D.C.: George Washington University, School of Education and Human Development, 1990.

Lenning, O. T., Sauer, L., and Beal, P. "Student Retention Strategies." In *Higher Education Research Reports.* No. 8. Washington, D.C.: ERIC Clearinghouse on Higher Education, 1980.

McPherson, M. S. *How Can We Tell If Federal Student Aid Is Working?* New York: College Board, 1988.

Malcom, S. "The Place of Minorities in the Scientific and Technical Workforce." *Black Scholar,* Sept.-Oct. 1985, pp. 50–55.

Mestre, J. P. "The Latino Science and Engineering Student: Recent Findings." In M. Olivas (ed.), *Latino College Students.* New York: Teachers College Press, 1986.

Mingle, J. R. *Focus on Minorities: Trends in Higher Education Participation and Success.* Denver, Colo.: Education Commission of the States/State Higher Education Executive Officers, 1987.

Mortenson, T. G. *Financial Aid Research Brief.* No. 7. Iowa City, Iowa: American College Testing Program, 1990.

Mortenson, T. G., and Wu, Z. *High School Graduation and College Participation of Young Adults by Family Income Backgrounds: 1970 to 1989.* Iowa City, Iowa: American College Testing Program, 1990.

Muñoz, D. "Identifying the Areas of Stress for Chicano Undergraduates." In M. Olivas (ed.), *Latino College Students.* New York: Teachers College Press, 1986.

Murdock, T. "It Isn't Just Money: The Effect of Financial Aid on Persistence." *Review of Higher Education,* 1987, *7* (1), 75–101.

National Association of Independent Colleges and Universities. *Independent Colleges and Universities: A National Profile.* Washington, D.C.: National Association of Independent Colleges and Universities, 1989.

National Institute of Independent Colleges and Universities. *A Commitment to Access: Undergraduate Student Financial Assistance Provided Directly by Independent Colleges and Universities.* Washington, D.C.: National Institute of Independent Colleges and Universities, 1990.

Nettles, M. "Racial Similarities and Differences in the Predictors of Student College Achievement." Paper presented at the annual meeting of the American Educational Research Association, Apr. 1984.

Olivas, M. *Latino College Students.* New York: Teachers College Press, 1986.

Pantages, T. J., and Creedon, C. F. "Studies of College Attrition: 1950–1975." *Review of Educational Research,* 1978, *48* (1), 49–101.

Peng, S. *Withdrawal from Institutions of Higher Education.* Washington, D.C.: National Center for Education Statistics, 1977.

Peng, S., and Fetters, W. B. "Variables Involved in Withdrawal During the First Two Years of College." *American Educational Research Journal,* 1978, *15* (3), 361–372.

Porter, J., Gregory, B., and Fenske, R. "Student Persistence and Financial Aid Packaging from Entry to Graduation: A Six-Year Longitudinal Study." In L. Berkener (ed.), *Proceedings of the 7th Annual Conference of the NASSGP/NCHELP Research Network.* Trenton: New Jersey Higher Education Assistance Authority, 1990.

Porter, O. F. "Persistence in Four-Year Colleges: Are There Differences in Public and Independent Institutions?" In L. Berkener (ed.), *Proceedings of the 7th Annual Conference of the NASSGP/NCHELP Research Network.* Trenton: New Jersey Higher Education Assistance Authority, 1990a.

Porter, O. F. *Undergraduate Completion and Persistence in Four-Year Colleges and Universities: Detailed Findings.* Washington, D.C.: National Institute of Independent Colleges and Universities, 1990b.

Stampen, J., and Cabrera, A. "Explaining the Effects of Student Aid in Attrition." *Journal of Student Financial Aid,* 1986, *16,* 28–40.

Stampen, J., and Cabrera, A. "The Targeting and Packaging of Student Aid and Its Effect on Attrition." *Economics of Education Review,* 1988, *7,* 15–27.

Stampen, J., and Fenske, R. "The Impact of Financial Aid on Ethnic Minorities." *Review of Higher Education,* 1988, *2* (4), 337–355.

Terkla, D. G. "Does Financial Aid Assure Undergraduate Persistence?" Paper presented at the ASHE/AERA meeting, San Francisco, Oct. 1984.

Tierney, M. L. "The Impact of Financial Aid on Student Demand for Public and Private Higher Education." *Journal of Higher Education,* 1980, *51,* 527–545.

Tinto, V. "Dropout from Higher Education: A Theoretical Synthesis of Recent Research." *Review of Educational Research,* 1975, *45,* 89–125.

Tinto, V. *Leaving College.* Chicago: University of Chicago Press, 1987.

Trent, J. W., and Medsker, L. *Beyond High School.* San Francisco: Jossey-Bass, 1968.

U.S. Department of Education, Office of Planning, Budget, and Evaluation. *The Escalating Costs of Higher Education.* Washington, D.C.: U.S. Department of Education, 1990.

Voorhees, R. A. "Financial Aid and Persistence: Do the Federal Campus-Based Aid Programs Make a Difference?" *Journal of Student Financial Aid,* 1985, *15,* 21–30.

Wolfle, L. "Postsecondary Educational Attainment Among Whites and Blacks." Paper presented at the annual meeting of the American Educational Research Association, Apr. 1983.

Woodward, C. "The Effects of Single-Year Scholarships Versus Renewable Scholarships on Student Persistence." *College and University,* 1988, *63* (2), 162–167.

Oscar F. Porter is assistant executive director of the National Institute of Independent Colleges and Universities.

INDEX

Abuses, program, 51, 52, 71
Academic merit, 9, 86
Access to higher education, 14, 67, 79, 82
Accountability. *See* Institutions, postsecondary; Regulations (loan program)
Accreditation agencies, roles of, 39-40
ACT. *See* American College Tests (ACT)
Administration, aid: changing demands of, 69-72; current factors influencing, 67-69; data maintenance commitments of, 17, 51, 52; philosophical foundation of, 65-66; processing and record-keeping burdens of, 13, 50-51, 59; staffing, 67, 72. *See also* Regulations (loan program)
Administrator, financial aid. *See* Financial aid administrator
Agencies, guarantee. *See* State-designated loan agencies
Aid, bases of student: academic merit, 9, 86; need, 9-10, 25, 34, 46-47, 79, 86. *See also* Need analysis
Aid delivery: history of, 4-6, 9-13, 44-46, 65-67, 69; streamlining of, 59-60; support services, 84-85. *See also* Administration, aid; Systems, student aid
Aid to Families with Dependent Children (AFDC), 54, 55
American College Tests (ACT), 11, 44
American Council on Education, 26, 27, 31
Application procedures (student aid): reapplication and, 59-60, 66; reasons to simplify, 50-51; standardization of, 49-50. *See also* Forms, aid application
Assets, parental, 25, 46, 56, 68. *See also* Family finances
Astin, A. W., 77, 88
Automation. *See* Computerization of student aid functions
Auxiliary Loans to Assist Students, 23

Banks. *See* Lenders, commercial
Basic Educational Opportunity Grant program, 5, 44. *See also* Pell Grants
Borrowers. *See* Student borrowers
Bosworth, Barry, 37
Budget Enforcement Act of 1930, 34
Burden, college costs. *See* Cost-sharing, higher education

Cabrera, A., 78-79, 89
Calculated need, 25
Calendar, regulations, 71
Campus-based programs. *See* Institutions, postsecondary
Cap, institutional default, 51
Capital markets, private. *See* Lenders, commercial
Certification standard, institutional (U.S.D.E.), 40
Choice. *See* Equality of educational opportunity
CM. *See* Congressional Methodology (CM)
Cohort rate, 38
Collection, loan, 15
College Entrance Examination Board, 44, 65
College savings bond programs, 29-30
College Scholarship Service (CSS), 11, 65-66
College Work-Study (CWS), 4, 7, 84, 86
Community colleges, two-year, 24, 26-27, 52, 62
Complexity of aid systems. *See* Simplification; Systems, student aid
Computerization of student aid functions, 40, 59-60, 68, 71, 72
Confidentiality, 66, 70
Congress. *See* U.S. Congress policies
Congressional Methodology (CM), 12, 25, 48, 56, 57; Pell Grants and, 48, 58-59
Contracts, tuition, 28-29
Contributions *vs.* award amounts, 58-59
Cost-sharing, higher education, 3-4; commercial loan risks and, 37-39; federal-state, 34-35, 85, 86; need for cooperation in, 33-34, 85-88; shifting burden of, 21-23, 77
Costs, college attendance, 65; differences among, 14, 18, 35, 67-68, 85-86; increases in, 22, 68, 77; prepayment of, 28-29

Costs, student loan: interest rates and, 15-17. *See also* Administration, aid
Counseling, student aid, 66-67, 69, 70, 72, 80
CSS. *See* College Scholarship Service (CSS)
CWS. *See* College Work-Study (CWS)

Data, applicant: accuracy and verification of, 45, 47, 50-51, 56-57, 61-62; complexity of, 70; confidentiality of, 66, 70; electronic processing of, 59-60; errors in, 45, 50, 56-57; federal simplification of, 49-50; integrating need analysis of, 57-59; multiple processing of, 11-13, 60, 66. *See also* Family finances; Forms, aid application
Data on educational institutions, 40; increase in required, 17, 51, 52-53; outcomes information, 41, 52
Data on student aid: insufficiency of, 8, 23; need for computerized, 40, 59-60, 68, 71, 72; NPSAS, 8-9, 24-25, 26-27; research on persistence and, 76-81; updating of, 60, 66. *See also* Statistics
Default rates (student loan), 23-24; of for-profit trade schools, 6, 24, 51-52; higher, 6, 15, 51, 61; institutional accountability for, 37-38, 71-72
Default-reduction policies: data verification and, 50-51, 61-62; selectivity of, 17. *See also* Regulations (loan program)
Degree completion. *See* Persistence (student)
Delivery. *See* Aid delivery; Systems, student aid
Demographics, changing student, 15, 23, 30, 50, 67, 70, 73, 83
Dependence, financial. *See* Independence
Disbursement, delayed, 52-53
Dropout. *See* Persistence (student)

Early intervention programs, 14, 36-37
Early tuition contracts, 28-29
Economy, U.S.: changes in the, 22-23
Education Amendments of 1986, 51
Education Department. *See* U.S. Department of Education
Educational Opportunity Grant Program, 4
Eligibility, institutional (U.S.D.E.), 39-41, 51, 61-62
Eligibility of applicants: simplifying the, 54
Enrollment, aid and, 68-69, 79
Environment, the college, 80, 81, 84
Equality of educational opportunity, 13-14, 43, 65, 75, 76-78, 79, 82
Equity: horizontal and vertical, 10; microequity and pair-wise, 46-47, 49; support for outcomes, 82-87; system simplicity *vs.*, 18-19, 45-47. *See also* Fairness issues
Errors, data, 45, 50, 56-57

Fairness issues: aid benefits and costs, 14; need analysis and, 10, 47
Family finances: assessment of, 10, 10-11, 18-19, 25, 46-47, 49, 57, 70; college savings plans and, 27-30, 69; complexity of, 68, 70-71; integrating need analysis of, 57-59; pair-wise comparisons of, 46-47, 49; parental assets and, 25, 46, 56, 68; reliance on, 25, 66, 77-78; simplified need analysis of, 49, 53-57; stagnation of, 22-23; student employment and, 26-27. *See also* Data, applicant; Need analysis
Federal government aid programs, 3-4; accountability and performance, 17, 49-53; college savings bonds, 29-30; expansion of, 6-8, 21-22, 67, 69; future policies of, 82-85; goals and beneficiaries of, 13-15, 43-44, 52, 75-76; history of, 4-6, 44-45; non-aid purposes of, 17; reinsurance of, 37-38; structure and balance of, 15-17. *See also* Regulations (loan program)
Fee, application, 12, 49
Fenske, R., 78-79, 80, 89
Financial aid administrators: changing demands on, 69-72; current roles of, 67-69; future roles of, 72-73; professional roles of, 65-67. *See also* Administration, aid
Fischer, F. J., 58-59
Fitzgerald, B. K., 56-57, 63
Forms, aid application: common and no-fee, 11, 12, 46, 49; complexity of, 50; updating, 60. *See also* Application procedures (student aid)
Formulas, need-analysis: current, 47-49; history of, 44-46; integration of, 57-59, 62; proposed, 54, 57-59; sensitivity of, 46-47. *See also* Need analysis
Front-loading of grants, 83-84

GI Bill, 4
Grants: proportion of loans to, 25, 33, 77, 83-84; statistics on, 9, 33
GSL. *See* Guaranteed Student Loans (GSL)
Guarantee agencies (loan). *See* State-designated loan agencies
Guaranteed Student Loans (GSL), 4-5. *See also* Stafford Student Loans
Guarantees, early, 14

Hansen, J. S., 23, 31
HEA. *See* Higher Education Act (HEA)
Hexter, H., 26, 31
High school performance, 80, 85
Higher Education Act (HEA), 82-83; increasing risk-sharing under the, 37-39; reauthorizations of the, 18, 25, 43, 57, 62, 76; Title IV programs, 48, 51, 63
Higher-income students, 70, 81, 85
History: of aid delivery, 4-6, 9-13, 44-46, 65-67, 69; of simplification efforts, 43-46, 48
Homemakers, displaced, 48, 57, 59
Hours, program credit and contact, 52
Human resource programs, recipients of federal, 54-55

ICL. *See* Income Contingent Loans (ICL)
Incentive funding, 34-37
Income cap for qualification, 54
Income Contingent Loans (ICL), 6
Independence, student financial, 23, 24, 70, 78-79
Independent institutions. *See* Private colleges and universities
Index, college costs, 35
Information. *See* Data on student aid
Institutions, postsecondary: accountability for default rates, 37-38, 51, 61, 71-72; accreditation of, 40; early-intervention roles of, 37; financial aid purposes of, 65-66, 80-81, 86-87; grant aid by, 33-34; higher default-rate, 51, 61; patterns of aid by, 7-9, 45, 67-68, 69-70; performance measures of, 17, 61-62; planning for aid at, 68-69, 72; student aid benefits to, 14; student employment patterns and, 26-27
Insurance, loan default, 15, 37-38
Integration of analysis. *See* Need analysis
Interest (student loans), 15-16. *See also* Lenders, commercial

Johnson administration, 4
Johnstone, D. B., 3, 19
Journal of Student Financial Aid, 58

Keppel Task Force. *See* National Task Force on Student Aid Problems

Lenders, commercial, 16-17, 69; guarantees to, 6, 8, 15, 37; increased risk-sharing by, 37-39
Licensing of schools, standards for, 40-41
Loans: proportion of grants to, 25, 33, 77, 83-84; statistics on, 9, 24
Lower-income students, 25, 48, 67, 71, 77, 80; need analysis exemptions for, 49, 54-55; Pell Grants for, 14, 18; program goals for, 49, 50, 79, 83

McPherson, M. S., 13, 19, 75, 88
Markets, capital. *See* Lenders, commercial
Matching programs (federal-state), 34-35, 85, 86; options for, 35-37
MDE. *See* Multiple data entry processors (MDE)
Measures: credit hour, 52; of family income, 10, 18-19, 25; institutional performance, 17, 61-62; lender performance, 39
Merit, aid and academic, 9, 86
Methodologies, need assessment. *See* Need analysis
Michigan Education Trust (MET), 28
Middle Income Student Assistance Act, 5, 16
Middle-income students, 22-23, 50, 62; aid for, 4, 14, 18
Minority students, 77, 80-81
Mortenson, T. G., 77, 83, 85, 89
Multiple data entry processors (MDE), 11, 12
Murdock, T., 79, 89

National Association of Financial Aid Administrators (NASFAA): Need Analysis Standards Committee, 54, 56
National Coalition for Coordination of Student Financial Aid, 12
National Defense Education Act (NDEA), 4
National Postsecondary Student Aid Survey (NPSAS), 8-9, 24-25, 26-27

National standards for licensing, 41
National student loan bank, 39
National Task Force on Student Aid Problems (Keppel Task Force), 11, 12, 45, 46
NDEA. *See* National Defense Education Act (NDEA)
Need analysis: current policy context of, 47-49; exempting groups from, 55; federal role in, 44-46; integration of, 57-59, 62; legislated simplifications of, 48-49; methodologies, 11-13; options for simplification of, 53-57; policy debates, 46-47, 81-82, 87-88; prediction factors, 54-55, 68-69, 71. *See also* Family finances; Formulas, need-analysis; Systems, student aid
Nonfederal sources of aid, 8-9. *See also* Institutions; Parents; State aid
NPSAS. *See* National Postsecondary Student Aid Survey (NPSAS)

Outcomes information, student: federally required, 17, 41; Uniform Methodology, 47. *See also* Persistence (student)
Overborrowing, issues of, 23-26
Oversight, components of federal, 39-41, 61, 71

Pair-wise comparisons. *See under* Equity
Paperwork (loan program), 17, 40, 59-60
Parent Loans for Undergraduate Students (PLUS), 6, 7, 8
Parents: college savings plans for, 27-30, 69; family assets and, 25, 46, 56, 68; financial support by, 9-10, 23, 66, 77-78
Partnership, federal-state-institutional, the: eligibility system and, 39-41; incentive funding and, 34-37; need for, 33-34, 41-42, 82, 86; risk-sharing by, 37-39
Pell Grants: Congressional Methodology and, 48, 58-59; data verification for, 49-50; eligibility for, 14-15, 18, 45; history of, 5, 22, 44, 48; increase in, 7, 22; NASFAA proposal for, 54, 56; proposed front-loading of, 83-84; separate methodology of the, 11, 12, 45. *See also* Basic Educational Opportunity Grant program
Perkins Loans (NDSL), 4, 6-8. *See also* National Defense Education Act (NDEA)
Persistence (student): future policies encouraging, 82-88; non-aid influences on, 80-81; research on student aid and, 76-79
Philosophy of financial aid administration, 65-66
Planning, institutional, 68-69, 72
PLUS. *See* Parent Loans for Undergraduate Students (PLUS)
Politicization, issues of, 17, 49, 57, 59, 61
Price Waterhouse, 56, 63
Private colleges and universities, 85, 86; federal student aid and, 9, 14, 46, 62, 69-70; working students in, 26-27
Private sector support, 87. *See also* Lenders, commercial
Proprietary trade schools. *See* Vocational or trade schools (for-profit)
Public colleges and universities: federal student aid in, 9, 24, 62, 69-70; income-based tuition for, 85-86; state-supported, 8

Quality control initiatives, 50-51

Reagan administration student aid policies, 5-6, 13
Reapplication data, updating, 59-60
Reauthorization. *See under* Higher Education Act
Redistribution, aid, 56-57
Re-entry students, 15, 48, 57, 58
Regulations (loan program): accountability and, 50-51, 71; the burden of, 17, 50-51, 59, 60-61, 68, 71; due-diligence, 38; federal scrutiny and, 17, 71; keeping up with, 68, 71; performance-based, 61-62, 71
Reinsurance of federal loans, 37-38
Research on persistence and student aid, 76-81
Retention, institutional, 17, 81, 87
Review, annual aid, 60, 66
Risk-sharing. *See* Lenders, commercial

Sector, institutional. *See* Institutions, postsecondary
SEOG. *See* Supplemental Education Opportunity Grants (SEOG)
Service, community, 27
Simplification: of aid application forms, 11, 46, 49; of application procedures,

49-51; implications of, 53, 55, 62; need analysis integration and, 57-59, 62; of need analysis models, 53-57; redistributional effects of, 56
SLS. *See* Supplemental Loans for Students (SLS)
Social Security, student aid from, 5, 7, 8, 21
Socioeconomic status, student, 80-81
Special allowance interest rate, 16
Special Services for Disadvantaged Students, 81
SSIG. *See* State Student Incentive Grants (SSIG)
Staffing, financial aid administration, 67, 72
Stafford Student Loans: availability of, 7, 8; defaults, 51, 71; delayed disbursement of first-time, 52-53; eligibility for, 25; increase in, 15, 23; separate application data for, 12-13, 59; subsidies, 15-16. *See also* Guaranteed Student Loans (GSL)
Stampen, J., 78-79, 80, 89
State aid: college savings bonds, 29-30; differences in, 35-36; endowment funds, 37; future policies of, 85-86; grant programs, 7, 8, 33, 36; matching programs, 34-37, 85, 86
State licensing for federal aid, 40
State Student Incentive Grants (SSIG), 5, 7, 34-35, 86; new purposes for, 35-37
State-designated loan agencies, 15, 37-38
Statistics: on available student aid, 6-9, 34-35, 67; data verification, 51; NPSAS, 8-9, 24-25, 26-27; student employment, 9, 26-27, 77
Stowe, P., 9, 19
Stress, student, 80-81
Student aid: effects of different types of, 76-78; effects on persistence, 78-79; philosophical basis of, 65-67; sources of, 3-4, 7-8, 69, 76-78; streamlining of, 12-13, 59-60. *See also* Grants; Loans; Work-study aid; *Names of individual programs*
Student aid administrators. *See* Financial aid administrators
Student borrowers: awards *vs.* contributions by, 58-59; defaulters among, 23-24; employment rates of, 26-27, 70; grants *vs.* loans to, 25, 33, 77, 83-84; increase in, 6-8, 21-22, 67; persistence of, 75-88; subpopulations of, 48, 54-55, 57, 58, 80; types of, 24-25, 48, 66-68, 70, 73. *See also* Lower-income students
Student Support Services program, 84-85
Students: aided *vs.* non-aided, 78-79; displaced homemakers, 48, 57, 59; financially independent, 23, 25, 70, 78-79; first-generation, 81; full-time, 27; growing diversity of, 15, 23, 30, 50, 67, 70, 73, 83; married, 58; military veteran, 4, 7, 8, 21; minority, 77, 80-81; part-time students, 15, 25; unemployed workers, 48, 57, 58; working, 26-27. *See also* Persistence (student)
Subsidies (Stafford Loan), 15-16
Supplemental Education Opportunity Grants (SEOG), 4, 7
Supplemental Loans for Students (SLS), 6, 7, 8, 51, 52
Supplemental Student Loans, 23
Systems, data. *See* Computerization of student aid functions
Systems, student aid: budget-driven, 42; calendar for, 71; evolution of, 9-13; market-basis of, 16-17, 37-39; need for automated, 59-60, 68, 71, 72; need-based, 25, 34, 46-47, 79, 86; options for simplifications of, 53-62; past simplifications of, 18, 46-47; performance assessment of, 61-62; unitary, 47, 48. *See also* Administration, aid

Tax credits, tuition, 4, 5
Taxation: income, 10, 55, 57, 68, 70; income too low for, 55; student aid system analogy to, 11, 43, 70-71; of tuition contracts, 28; of U.S. Savings Bonds, 30
Taxpayers, aid by. *See* Federal government aid programs; State aid
Technology. *See* Computerization of student aid functions
Tinto, V., 79, 81, 90
Title IV programs, 48, 51, 63
Trade schools. *See* Vocational or trade schools (for-profit)
Triad of federal programs (grant, loan, work), 4-5

Triad oversight process (federal aid), 39–41
TRIO strategies, 84–85
Tuition. *See* Costs, college attendance

U.S. Congress policies, 48, 50, 52, 71. *See also* Federal government aid programs
U.S. Department of Education, 11, 21–22, 40, 48, 50–51; data, 60, 77–78; performance assessment project, 61. *See also names of programs*
U.S. Savings Bonds, 29–30
UM. *See* Uniform Methodology (UM)
Unemployed workers, 48, 57, 58
Uniform Methodology (UM), 11, 46, 57

Verification. *See under* Data, applicant
Veterans. *See* Students
Vocational or trade schools (for-profit): federal student aid to, 9, 14–15, 34, 41, 62; loan default rates at, 6, 24, 51–52; working students in, 26–27

Women students, 48, 57, 59
Work-study aid, 9, 77, 85; College Work-Study (CWS), 4, 7, 84, 86
Wu, Z., 77, 83, 89

Zero contributions by students, 58
Zero-coupon bonds, 29
Zero-filling of forms, 49

Ordering Information

New Directions for Higher Education is a series of paperback books that provides timely information and authoritative advice about major issues and administrative problems confronting every institution. Books in the series are published quarterly in Fall, Winter, Spring, and Summer and are available for purchase by subscription as well as by single copy.

Subscriptions for 1991 cost $45.00 for individuals (a savings of 20 percent over single-copy prices) and $60.00 for institutions, agencies, and libraries. Please do not send institutional checks for personal subscriptions. Standing orders are accepted.

Single copies cost $13.95 when payment accompanies order. (California, New Jersey, New York, and Washington, D.C., residents please include appropriate sales tax.) Billed orders will be charged postage and handling.

Discounts for quantity orders are available. Please write to the address below for information.

All orders must include either the name of an individual or an official purchase order number. Please submit your order as follows:
Subscriptions: specify series and year subscription is to begin
Single copies: include individual title code (such as HE1)

Mail all orders to:
Jossey-Bass Inc., Publishers
350 Sansome Street
San Francisco, California 94104

For sales outside of the United States contact:
Maxwell Macmillan International Publishing Group
866 Third Avenue
New York, New York 10022

OTHER TITLES AVAILABLE IN THE
NEW DIRECTIONS FOR HIGHER EDUCATION SERIES
Martin Kramer, Editor-in-Chief

HE73 Using Consultants Successfully, *Jon F. Wergin*
HE72 Administrative Careers and the Marketplace, *Kathryn M. Moore, Susan B. Twombly*
HE71 Managing Change in Higher Education, *Douglas W. Steeples*
HE70 An Agenda for the New Decade, *Larry W. Jones, Franz Nowotny*
HE69 Financial Planning Under Economic Uncertainty, *Richard E. Anderson, Joel W. Meyerson*
HE67 Achieving Assessment Goals Using Evaluation Techniques, *Peter J. Gray*
HE66 Improving Undergraduate Education in Large Universities, *Carol H. Pazandak*
HE65 The End of Mandatory Retirement: Effects on Higher Education, *Karen C. Holden, W. Lee Hansen*
HE64 Successful Strategic Planning: Case Studies, *Douglas W. Steeples*
HE63 Research Administration and Technology Transfer, *James T. Kenny*
HE62 Making Computers Work for Administrators, *Kenneth C. Green, Steven W. Gilbert*
HE61 Leaders on Leadership: The College Presidency, *James L. Fisher, Martha W. Tack*
HE60 Increasing Retention: Academic and Student Affairs Administrators in Partnership, *Martha McGinty Stodt, William M. Klepper*
HE59 Student Outcomes Assessment: What Institutions Stand to Gain, *Diane F. Halpern*
HE58 Financing Higher Education: Strategies After Tax Reform, *Richard E. Anderson, Joel W. Meyerson*
HE57 Creating Career Programs in a Liberal Arts Context, *Mary Ann F. Rehnke*
HE56 Managing Programs for Learning Outside the Classroom, *Patricia Senn Breivik*
HE55 Crisis Management in Higher Education, *Hal Hoverland, Pat McInturff, C. E. Tapie Rohm, Jr.*
HE54 Institutional Revival: Case Histories, *Douglas W. Steeples*
HE53 Managing College Enrollments, *Don Hossler*
HE52 Making the Budget Process Work, *David J. Berg, Gerald M. Skogley*
HE51 Incentive for Faculty Vitality, *Roger G. Baldwin*
HE47 Leadership Roles of Chief Academic Officers, *David G. Brown*
HE45 Women in Higher Education Administration, *Adrian Tinsley, Cynthia Secor, Sheila Kaplan*